THE ' OF LIGHT

A PRAYER BOOK
FOR
PILGRIMS
ON THEIR WAY
TO
ETERNAL LIFE

Michael Radford

Believe in Divine Providence!

This book is dedicated to those
into whose hands it might fall
by the grace of God.

May it help you, dear Reader
towards the love of
Our Lord Jesus Christ
and
Our Blessed Lady.

If you believe, anything is possible.
(Mark 9:23)

Published in Great Britain by
Pen Press
25 Eastern Place
Brighton
BN2 1GJ

ISBN 978-1-906206-45-1

Printed and bound by Thomson Litho, East Kilbride

A catalogue record of this book is available from
the British Library

First published privately in the United Kingdom by the author in December 2006 as limited pilot edition of 20 copies. Revised in March 2007 by a proof edition of 25 copies.

This edition produced using the services of Pen Press Publishers Ltd, 25 Eastern Place, Brighton BN2 1GJ

2nd Impression   December 2007

4th Impression   March 2009

Typesetting and origination by Michael Radford.

12 pt. print size for those with eyesight that needs it!

The author's material is rendered in

Times New Roman font.

All other material in set in this Arial font.

BY THE SAME AUTHOR

The Alvis 12/50 Engine

The Vintage Alvis Manual

Acknowledgements

I believe that God the Holy Spirit prompted me to write this book and to use the talents God gave me for His service in helping lead souls to heaven. Thank you Lord for making use of me in my old age and in giving me the joy of writing this book.

I acknowledge the help and encouragement of wise friends amongst the clergy, especially Rev. Father Patrick Sayles S.S.C. (The Prayer Trust).

A number of my relations and friends suggested prayers for "The Gloria of Prayers" section and have given advice about the text. Chris Busk helped me get all the text onto a disk fit for the publisher's use. I am deeply indebted to them all and very grateful to have such friends.

The author thanks the following for their gracious permission to reproduce material from their writings:

Teresa M Orton   —   A Modern Day Fable - Retirement.
The Prayer Trust   —   Prayers –   Everything We Do
                                         Befriend me Holy Spirit
                                         First and final prayer of
                                         The Way of the Cross.
      and the following for their art work:

Pippa Kearon   —   The Cover Illustration
Tara Cullinan   —   The Stations of the Cross
Mary Cox   —   Wayside Cross

Back Page Image:
Sr. Columba   —   Peace Begins with a Smile

Contents

How the Way is Lit

The Rosary Way

A Gloria of Prayers

The Way of the Cross

The Way to God

Author's Preface

Pilgrims! We are on a journey from life to death, the gateway to eternal life. If we believe and trust in Jesus to save us, we will be amongst the Saints who pass into heaven. The Good Thief trusted Jesus saying "Jesus remember me when you come into your kingdom," and Jesus replied — "To-day, you will be with me in paradise."

For most of us the journey seems long. We are easily distracted from our goal and from the safest route by the attractions of this world. Some may even doze at the wheel. This is a 'Wake Up' call. Pull in; take a break to take stock. Satellite navigation won't steer us along our way to eternal life. We won't find guidance on the internet or be advised by mobile phone talk.

The true guidance system we do have is Living Light! Contact the Source of Living Light by prayer. Read about prayer within these pages.

"I am the light of the world, so if you follow me, you won't be stumbling in the darkness for Living Light will flood your path."

(John 8:12)

Michael Radford
Brighton, Sussex. 2007 AD

P.S.   Our First Prayer dear reader!

Pray for me, and I shall pray for you and all your friends that we may merrily meet in heaven.

(Saint Thomas More's last letter to his daughter, Meg)

Preamble

Some years ago my wife Audrey gave me a prayer book for Christmas titled *Living Light* which words are taken from the verse of St. John's gospel (8:12) quoted in the Preface. Everything good that occurs in my life happens by Divine Providence such as the somewhat unusual present of the little prayer book. Treasuring this prayer book greatly, I had hoped to be able to make a Christmas gift of it to several of my 'Co-worker of Mother Teresa' friends who have given us great practical and prayer support during Audrey's suffering with dementia. Sadly the book is out of print and will remain so.

Often when good thoughts come, they seem to be inspired and given from an inner source. I believe this is how the Holy Spirit showers out Divine Providence. Whilst lying in bed at about 3am on 29th March 2006, a few days after my 82nd birthday, a kaleidoscope of beautiful thoughts was turning in my mind. Worried that recall would escape me later, I got up and made some notes to remind me of what had, I believe, really been put there by the Holy Spirit. There was enough material on the theme of *Living Light* to start writing an alternative prayer book but of a very different kind. The Holy Spirit gives different people different languages to speak the message of the marvels of God.

Hopefully with thanks to Divine Providence, I will be given the time to complete this book and benefit the prayer life of my friends and others as well.

Completion of this book is properly acknowledged at its end by my last two words of text (p.117) – have a look!

9

HOW

THE WAY

IS LIT

A Pilgrim's Way

This book is for pilgrims on the way to everlasting life who find they have reached a fork in the road ahead and realise they need guidance. Many circumstances in life may cause this, such as a change of job, an accident, retirement, bereavement, a broken relationship or the onset of illness. 'A Modern Day Fable – Retirement' written by Teresa Orton tells the story of one person but mirrors our own lives at one stage or another:-

Once there was a woman. She was neither young nor old. It depended on your perspective of age or which shaft of sunlight was shining when you met her. The woman was travelling along the road with her companions; loving; laughing and living life to the full. But she had noticed that the back-pack she was carrying was getting heavy and making her back ache.

The journey began to get a bit tiresome; brambles from the hedgerows reached out and snagged her arms. Branches from the low-hung trees brushed her head irritating her. It seemed to her that everyone else on the road was now hurrying faster, noisily insisting on getting there; wherever 'there' was. The more she plodded the more her back ached. Her companions were sympathetic and offered to take turns in helping her, but each was carrying their own pack. She knew that this was not the answer.

So she decided to stop by the wayside and rest for a while. As she sat there she looked back down the road. It had been a tough one at times, but still a happy one. There had been stretches of straight road and good weather that had made up for the rocky parts and stormy weather. She and her companions had coped, together and yet singularly. Feeling better for the rest, the woman stood up to shoulder her back-pack again. But suddenly the road ahead forked into a crossroads. To the left in the distance she could hear the voices of her companions but to the right … where had that road come from? She had not noticed it before. It meandered over a bridge but it was impossible to see what lay beyond. Not even the flowers or the trees seemed to be the same.

Then a long-ago memory stirred. A friend had told her these cross roads would appear but she had ignored it blithely. It had seemed so long ago and now it was here. When she stood hesitating, a voice spoke rudely over her shoulder: "Hey, you! Young-old woman. Will you make up your mind! There are people behind you, you know!"

Shrinking back out of the way of the crowd she thought fearfully, "Oh no, I can't make up my mind so quickly. Maybe I'd better stay on the side until I can make up my mind." As she sat there twisting her hands and crying in her heart, a woman came and sat down beside her. She too was a young-old woman and looked familiar.

"Do I know you?"

"Of course" smiled the newcomer. "I am your wisdom. Your own particular being of knowledge whom you acquired over the years, not only from your own experiences but from each person you have met. I am here to help you decide which road, the one familiar or the one less known."

"Well" the woman admitted, "It is scary just because it is so new to me." Her new friend smiled sympathetically. "Why did you think it was getting difficult to travel? It wasn't the road. It was you. You were ready for change. Like a chrysalis your surroundings were becoming uncomfortable. This my dear, is a new way. It is not a terminal station. Just a new challenge."

"But I can't see the signposts or any indications of what it will be like."

"Did you know the way when you started, way back when? It was just as new and the sign posts just as unclear and you are forgetting two important things."

"What are they?" Hope was beginning to stir. "Firstly, you are a seasoned traveller. You have learned much along the way. You know how to weather the storms and to find the smoothest paths. Secondly, you will not be alone. I will be with you and I carry the lantern gathered in your pioneering days and others will be glad to travel with you because of the light you will be sharing."

So the young-old woman bent to pick up her back-pack to take the right turn but her companion stopped her. "You will need a lighter one now. Just empty out all the things you needed till now. Others will come along and take what they require for their needs." And even though it was the right thing to do, it hurt her right through to her bones.

"I can't do it. It will break my heart."

"Of course you can; hearts don't break over things. The joy of having them is already in your inner self. All you are doing is casting off excess weight."

So she closed her eyes tightly and emptied out her back-pack. In a very short while it was all gone and her companion was right. The load was much lighter.

"See" she smiled, "You can only celebrate the past when you embrace the future."

So the young-old woman and her companion started off together, taking the road that led over the bridge.

I really felt for the woman in this fable and tried to analyse why. Firstly, getting rid of life's useless clutter, bric-a-brac and an excess of clothes I've found is liberating and you can't take a penny coin with you into the next life. Secondly, I liked the woman's alter ego… "I am your wisdom." As a cradle

Catholic, I learnt a long time ago that Wisdom was one of the seven gifts of the Holy Spirit and being wise like King Solomon would make me more comfortable with myself and my friends and relations when they seek my advice. Thirdly, it was equally comforting to be told that … "others will be glad to travel with you because of the light you will be sharing."

Hence I have used Teresa Orton's really compelling words to introduce this chapter. However, the main message of the tale is "Take stock and act accordingly." Where is one amassing one's treasures – on earth or in heaven? The recent television programmes on "The Monastery" and "The Convent" each showed five men and four women in turn seeking sanctuary there and taking stock of their lives with unexpected results for the worldly wise. If you peel back all the skins of your temporal being, you will find you have a spiritual core at its centre.

Now, this pilgrim will tell you how he came to write a third book with such a strange mix of topic to the first two he had written. Writing all three have had a common motivation, namely my desire to pass on the benefits of my experience in solving certain problems I've met in life. My recent problems have been of a very different kind hence the disparate mix of subject matter. My purpose in even listing my earlier books is not to 'Trumpet Blow' but to make a confession and clear my conscience over a jocular misquote in "The Alvis 12/50 Engine" book now related.

From an early age motor cars fascinated me as they did Toad in The Wind in the Willows, by Kenneth Grahame (1908). I volunteered for the army in 1942 to ensure I served in The Royal Armoured Corps so that I could pursue my interest in mechanical vehicles and to avoid route marches and to be safe from rifle bullets! In 1952 at the age of twenty-eight I became the proud owner of a vintage Alvis twelve-fifty motor car and then joined the Alvis club catering for these cars. By 1999 I had written two books relating to their care and upkeep to benefit a readership of about 600. In the Alvis 12/50 Engine book I told how my younger brother David knocked down the wall of a cottage he owned to garage my Alvis whilst I was on service in Malaya and added — 'Greater love no man hath than he who knocks down the walls of his property to house his brother's 12/50.' To my shame I didn't realise whose words I was misquoting — 'Please forgive me Lord.'

As an aside, I am proud to say that my elder brother John, on the retreat to Dunkirk, did lay down his life for friends in his infantry section. He covered their withdrawal from enemy attack by firing his Bren gun from the hip. The villagers of nearby Pelves in France recovered his and two of his comrades' bodies and buried them in their own cemetery. They have tended the graves lovingly ever since. On every Liberation Day 8th May (VE Day) the bravery of the three English soldiers is honoured with great ceremony.

Thus many spare time hours of my working life and early retirement was spent on writing two books on how to care for Vintage Alvises. Recently the owners of my rented garage sold the block of garages for property development so my Alvis had to be sold. I am now free of its materialistic entrapment which has proved a moral and spiritual benefit to me and my wife Audrey. Audrey suffers from dementia which started with slight memory loss about five years ago. Her speech has steadily deteriorated during the past three years to become mostly unrecognisable jargon but varying tones of voice do communicate moods. For some time she has been unable to read or write or watch television. Let's face the truth, caring for lumps of metal and those we love at the same time are not compatible when the latter proves to be a full time task that requires human and spiritual back-up and a constant updating of one's caring skills. So, in a strange way, the enforced selling of my Alvis hobby horse was heaven sent or happened by 'Divine Providence.'

Nearly three years ago Audrey's sleep patterns started to go haywire and nights became times of frantic concern. In the first instance to calm my own nerves, I took to saying the Rosary at bedtime which calmed me down after any stress during the day whilst the prescription of a sleeping pill for Audrey regulated her sleep patterns. Some thoughts on saying the Rosary are given later.

Dementia strikes one in five people over the age of eighty and there is no cure for this illness. There are some 750,000 persons so afflicted in the UK. There are said to be about a hundred different forms of dementia and Alzheimer's disease accounts for about 60% of the total sufferers. There are various forms of support systems which are not the subject of this book. But nearly all sufferers are looked after by an elderly spouse or other family members. These persons are known as carers.

I started attending a monthly meeting for carers run by the local Alzheimer's Society. After several meetings I began to find these a bit irksome and was going to say at the next meeting that I was unable to come any more. However, two other carers in the group welcomed me warmly saying how glad they were to see me as they found my various comments and example of great value. They added they didn't know how I managed to cope so well when clearly my problems were a stage worse than theirs. As taking my rosary out of my pocket and telling them saying the rosary was my way of coping would have meant nothing to them, I decided to say nothing on prayer but to continue attending the meetings. Then the inspiration came early one morning, just as told in the

Preamble, to write a prayer book for carers and others who feel they have an inexplicable void in their lives or feel a need to 'take stock.' 'Where am I going, what am I doing with my life?'

Jesus no doubt spent much of his life from the age of twelve to the start of his public life at the age of thirty working with St. Joseph in the carpenter's workshop thus sanctifying the work of human hands. Those in work and with busy family lives should offer up their work and lives each day as an active form of prayer, dedication and worship of God. Doing the proper works of life well has wonderful merit. Having lived in Salisbury in the 1930s, the Cathedral church of the Blessed Virgin Mary with its elegant and glorious spire rising to 404 feet, lifts up a wonderful prayer to God of the work of human hands. It still casts a spiritual spell for all to see for miles around nearly seven hundred years after the last stone was laid.

The 'fly in the ointment' today is that in an affluent society we have the means to live the good life and to live it up and most of us become grossly acquisitive. We finish sitting on the pile we have made and with a back-pack of needless and useless rubbish perhaps even with a hoard of 'cash in the attic' for our progeny to squabble over. The fable at the start of this chapter is an early warning. Some of us may learn from the jolt of retirement whilst others like myself, need a more severe shock. God wants us all in heaven because He loves us. His way of getting us there is not our choice of way which is usually the soft option.

We are all on a pilgrimage — we are on our 'Way' and we need 'Light' and it is my belief that prayer brings the spiritual light we need for the journey hence this book's title 'THE WAY OF LIGHT.' It is a collection of thoughts on prayer coupled to formal prayers and those from the heart that I have found helpful in my new found role as a full time carer. But, we are all called to be carers of our neighbour and to wash each other's feet.

"I give you a new commandment,
Love one another as I have loved you!"
(John 13:34)

The first step on the Way of Light is to love one another as Jesus loved His disciples and His neighbour — and who was that? He told them in the parable of the Good Samaritan who gave help to one of the most foolish men imaginable but did not judge or ignore him as some others had. The idiot had risked travelling alone on the road from Jerusalem to Jerico, a road notorious for footpads and cutthroats.

Jesus then led by example in curing the lepers, healing the sick, casting out devils, feeding the hungry, giving sight to the blind, raising the dead and forgiving sins and most notably asking forgiveness for His executioners — "Father, forgive them, for they know not what they do." The gospels are full of stories of His loving kindness, compassion and wonderful words.

The example He gave was of Divine Providence in action, and how all can be Good Samaritans in their own time and place — and moreover to be ready to forgive those who trespass against them.

He ran out and embraced him.
(Luke 15:20)

Divine Providence and Justice

The souls of the Just are in the hands of God.

(Wisdom 3:1)

When Divine Providence seems to be taking a hand in answer to prayers and work to give Justice to others, the finger of God can be seen in this by those given light.

The purpose of this chapter is to show the reader pointers which prove that there is a Divine Providence that watches over each and every one of us every moment of every day. God is love and loves every individual person with an infinite and everlasting love. To be aware of this truth and to see God at work among us will bring a peace and comfort that the world cannot bring. God sent His only son Jesus Christ into this sinful world as one of us to redeem us from our sins by His passion, death and resurrection. This is the central tenet of a belief in Divine Providence. We are saved from our sins simply by belief in Jesus and trusting Him to save us. Remember that most of Our Lord's miracles were worked for those who had faith and believed in Him.

Furthermore, throughout our lives God cares for us with His blessings and graces that provide light to guide our way. His chief blessing is the gift of His Holy Spirit living within us who guides our prayer and prays within us for everything we need in accordance with God's holy will. Other blessings are the talents we are given, loving friendships we make, and beneficent circumstances that occur in our lives that make for our sanctification. Indeed Divine Providence provides us with blessings and graces day after day countless in their number. It is God's light that reveals His acts of providence to us so that we can learn to rely on Him with faith in His Providence and thank Him for His blessings.

There are very many people in the world who think they have reason to claim there is no such thing as Divine Providence. They say that a good and loving God would not permit large scale evil and disaster to take place. To answer this and to look at the obverse of the coin, let us consider evil or disaster firstly on the scale of one person from a religious point of view. Jesus told us that we do not know the day or the hour when we will be called to eternal life but that we must be ready. Death for some occurs after a long illness allowing some warning but others are called quite suddenly. A single death by accident or evil cause is a tragedy to the nearest and dearest who sometimes begin to doubt God's goodness and providence. A large number of deaths, due to some form of catastrophe in one locality, makes many say "How can God allow this?" or "I don't believe there can be a God for this to happen." There are even those who cite this as proof that there is no God. We are talking here of cases of earthquake, fire, flood, war, atrocities and other such events in the world. The Boxing Day tsunami of 2004 is one of these frightening circumstances or the terrorist atrocities named 9/11 and 7/7. However, the average death rate for the whole world is a staggering 156,712 persons daily (57.2 million per year). Thus catastrophic deaths of groups here and there are not extreme when seen in context of world deaths. It is the scale of deaths on 9/11, 7/7 and 12/26 in one locality caused by one specific disaster that shocks humanity so deeply. Notwithstanding, all were aware "they did not know the day or the hour" and they were told to be ready and the ones that were ready, simply happened to be in the same place at the same time with the others who weren't. Is Divine Providence still watching over humanity on such days? Let us think on this. Every circumstance of suffering in this world brings out the best from those who have heard and listened to the words of Jesus -

"Love one another as I have loved you."

Certainly, victims of such tragedies are prayed for more generously than would have been the case had they slipped away quietly unbeknown to the world except by their close relatives. Furthermore, in all these most tragic cases, a vast number of people around the world woke up to the fact their neighbour was in trouble on the other side of the road and became Good Samaritans with relief help of one form or another. Thus a proportion of the witnesses become better people as a result of witnessing a tragic and sad event. What has Divine Providence got to do with these matters? The Holy Spirit working within our being urges us on to show love and compassion to the afflicted. If you suffer these feelings, you have not grown soft, your God-given human nature is responding to a prompt from Divine Providence to love and serve your neighbour. Thus, out of what appears to be an evil, good may flower and often does. Almighty God might be seen to be giving humanity a wake-up call. Providential?

Other problems, such as the building of towns on flood plains, are caused by the greed of developers which is against Justice to those desperate for housing. Likewise, building or re-building cities on the earth's crust fault lines or near to volcanoes cannot be construed as proof there is no God when a natural law finally operates. Humanity ignored wake-up calls in Biblical times and God gave Noah the tip to build the Ark! Here we do have evidence of Divine Providence at work. But, God did not postpone the flood. God allows the universe and nature to develop and evolve according to his laws some of which are not fully understood. "My ways are not your ways" — God does not tinker around with his creation and its systems just because lowly human beings think the design is faulty. The make-up of our planet and its fragile eco systems demands that we act as good caretakers for future generations and do not misuse God's gifts. Uneven distribution of God's gifts over the planet results in terrible suffering in Third World countries which need help to correct this by rich nations. Often political factions in poorer nations try to solve their economic problems by armed conflict using arms they buy from the richest nations. Thus the greedy rich profit from the killing. This is an obscene affront to Justice and yet the rich have the means to provide a fairer share of Divine Providence to those who need it. Many such tragedies are caused by the forces of devil driven evil that is man's injustice to his fellow man — don't blame God or suggest there is no God.

Racism, one of the scourges of humanity from time immemorial, causing hatred and discrimination and 'Man's inhumanity to man,' reached an extreme limit during the Holocaust years of the Second World War. Whilst more recent 'Ethnic Cleansing' shows these old ills of society still persist. Racism is a human evil and God the Son has given us the cure for that:

Love one another as I have loved you.

St. Peter's and the Apostles' experiences have a lesson for us relating to more recent events. Whilst netting fish in Lake Galilee, Jesus recruits Simon (Peter) and his brother Andrew 'to catch men.' A little further on He meets James and John in their boat getting their nets ready and they also join Him. Some of the topics of the time no doubt were religion, politics and work — the hated Romans, and the corrupt Temple dealers. Throwing in their lot with Jesus, the long heralded Saviour, they feel sure they will be in the vanguard of a movement for 'Regime Change.' Everything goes well for three years. Peter even realises that Jesus is the Son of God. They all see Jesus as the saviour of the Jewish race. Then, when it seems likely Jesus will be apprehended, Peter arms himself with a sword to act as His bodyguard. They think Jesus, the miracle worker, will somehow bring down the establishment.

Everything, in their view, goes tragically wrong when Jesus submits peaceably to His captors as a lamb led to the slaughter. Peter, to save his own skin, denies he is one of Jesus' disciples. The supposed long-awaited saviour of the Jewish race undergoes a mock-up trial meekly, is almost flogged to death, then crowned with thorns and made to carry His cross to the place of execution by crucifixion. He dies on the cross and is buried in a borrowed tomb nearby. Yes, everything has gone terribly and devastatingly wrong.

The next scene is of two of Jesus' disciples making their way from Jerusalem to Emmaus. Jesus falls in with them but they do not recognise Him. "What are you talking about?" He asks. "You must be the only person who does not know what has happened. Jesus, in whom we believed, was crucified and on the third day rose from the dead." Their companion, the Divine Wayfarer, then tells them how the scriptures and prophets had foretold that "The Christ would have to suffer to save the human race from their sins." They ask Jesus in for a meal and recognise Him "At the breaking of Bread." He disappears and they chase back to Jerusalem to tell Peter and the others they have met the Lord. Finally the message strikes home that the Christ had not come to effect regime change in Palestine. At last they accept the real truth that the Christ came to save all of those who believe in the name of Jesus from their sins. That Justice is brought about by obeying His new Commandment "Love one another as I have loved you." Thus Jesus commands us to be Co-workers of the triune God as Instruments of Divine Providence using our God-given talents. Hence the love of Justice comes from God alone.

Your reading of this book at this moment is the result of Divine Providence and to persuade you of this I will tell you two separate stories about myself. Firstly how I came to believe so firmly in Divine Providence and then how I became competent enough to set pen to paper in this way.

Thirty years ago when Audrey and myself settled in Brighton as Co-workers of Mother Teresa from Kent, we were immediately enrolled on the Sussex Committee by Mrs Bunty Watts who had been a founder member of the Co-workers in Calcutta working directly with Mother Teresa. One of Mother Teresa's strict rules for her Missionaries of Charity and her Co-workers was that there should be no commercial fund-raising and that the work must rely solely on Divine Providence. After a few years I became Sussex Treasurer and the funds rolled in without any fund raising graft — I thought of myself as 'The Big Fisherman.' Another of Mother's wishes was that her Co-workers throughout the world should seek out the poorest of the poor in their own localities and care for them in any way possible. Thus we became committee members of St. Anne's Day Centre for Homeless and Lonely People in Kemptown, Brighton. In December 2000 I was appointed Treasurer and asked that we adopt the No Fund Raising policy and rely solely on Divine Providence. Basically this means accepting finance and gifts from charitable sources, parishes etc. and individuals. Even I knew we needed quite a lot of Divine Providence — more in fact than had been provided up to then! We had to trust the Lord to provide! The Chairman and the Secretary (Mike and Heather Kearon) were sceptical but agreed to my request as they were desperate for a treasurer. After six years we are still solvent and have been a Charitable Trust for three years. Volunteers to serve on the committee and to help run the Day Centre have come forward willingly. By Divine

Providence our ship had weathered a number of storms. Recently Mike said to me "Mick, you've taught us one thing in our time together — we believe in Divine Providence." I've two converts so far but am hoping for many more.

Our dearest and closest friend in Brighton (well — Hove, actually!) is Paddy Hughes — Mrs Dorothy Patricia! She is also the dearest and closest friend of many other people. She told me recently that her jobbing builder who came to mend a crack in a wall called her Victorian terraced house 'The Sanctuary.' When Audrey's illness started to become worse, Paddy asked to take care of her every Friday at 'The Sanctuary' from 10am when the three of us would have a cup of coffee and biscuit together. This practice started on Friday 11th June 2004 (St. Barnabas Apostle). Paddy and I always had a good chat. When I started showing her my draft copies of the first pages of this book in these moments, she said she wanted to read about my thoughts on Divine Providence so these are they. Then I would go home to get on with things. At four I would return to Paddy's for what would be called in olden days 'High Tea' with several other Co-worker friends. All Co-workers are friends who help each other practically when they can and by prayer anyway. When the role of full-time carer came my way, it was surprising how many instruments of Divine Providence I met. I believe we are all called to be instruments of Divine Providence in our own ways. The basis for this belief has been the example given by Blessed Teresa of Calcutta.

On reflection, Divine Providence has also been at work throughout my life keeping me safe and sound to the age of eighty-three regardless of being a tank troop leader in India and the Burma campaign. After a week in India during squadron training in the wilds, my General Grant tank with the complete crew of seven nearly drove into a vast artesian well. By Divine Providence I saw the danger just in time to avert the catastrophe of myself and crew being drowned. Five years later my Guardian Angel saw me safely through the 3-day Battle of the Imgin in the Korean War. There have been other major hazards of life such as owning a motor cycle for three years with one miraculous escape from certain death thanks to my Guardian Angel, my servant of Divine Providence. Now comes the second part of my story of how I became a proficient wordsmith.

I was educated at Ratcliffe College by the Rosminians of the Institute of Charity. On studying for the School Certificate of those days, all of us wished fervently to be in Brother Basil Roche's English classes. We knew we were in for a very hard time with him because he stood for no nonsense whatever although he rarely sent a pupil out for punishment of the old fashioned variety. His discipline was the work he set us and the fair marking he gave. All boys like to rib their teachers but this was a no-go area with Rocker Roche! Why did we want to suffer so? Brother Roche never had a single failure in the School Certificate English examination in all his years teaching and many of his pupils including myself got Credits in English Language and Literature. The first bricks of my own story as a writer and survivor are in place.

During my time in the army, I had a job for four years of testing Service vehicles and the follow-up report writing. This gave practice in Military Writing where one has to marshal the facts and set them down in a lucid fashion. This was another brick in the wall of word-smithing. Enjoying the fun and discipline of writing as well as running my Alvis for both work and play, I started writing lengthy Instruction Books to benefit my friends in the Alvis Club which concluded in 1999.

Notwithstanding, here was a competent author who, the Lord saw, was out of work. But, perhaps He had been preparing me to serve Him in an unexpected way in order to write this book. Force of circumstances or Providence decreed that I sold my Alvis thus clearing the decks for action. As a sop to this loss, I've made a new friend, Peter, a taxi-driver in Hove who has recently purchased a 1927 Alvis and he often rings me up for a lengthy talk and advice from the 'Man who wrote the Alvis Bible!' This keeps me mentally active and gives me recreation in a well known sphere. God is good!

For over thirty years as Co-workers of Mother Teresa, Audrey and I had prayed the Co-workers prayer whenever we met our Co-worker friends and said prayers for various intentions. "Make me a Channel of your peace" is one line of this prayer. I cannot imagine how many people will find the words in this book helpful to them but writing them is a vocation for me. If you are under stress, or troubled in mind and not at peace with yourself, the answer is not to light another cigarette, eat chocolate, to take a shot of alcohol or resort to retail therapy but to pray. Say the Lord's Prayer with all one's heart and soul and Divine Providence will give immediate comfort and peace – prayer has no ill side effects like Valium or similar drug! A longer prayer is often needed to give the mind a clean and larger break from stress raising thoughts. Saying the Rosary answers this need and the better you pray it, the greater the peace you receive. I promise that you will derive peace from prayer and especially when saying the Rosary. It gets easier to say as time passes and it becomes part of yourself. If you turn to prayer, my own prayer will be answered – the Lord will have indeed made me a channel of His peace for another person. If there is a sea change in your life, you might even say to yourself — "reading this book has got me into thinking I must learn to trust in Divine Providence!"

The Lord uses strange instruments; His first Pope was an uneducated fisherman until he met "The Lord and Saviour of Mankind." Truth is stranger than fiction for who would ever believe that a military writer and vintage car enthusiast would be prompted at the sunset of life to write a book such as this.

I struggled for some time over a title and kicked around a lot of stilted ideas in my mind but all to no good. Then a flash of Divine Inspiration came early on the morning of 19th June 2006 suggesting "THE WAY OF LIGHT." This is clearly the perfect title. You can't escape sensing the action of Divine Providence when your eyes are opened.

My last story illustrates how Divine Providence operates so very obviously. I am citing the most recent one that happened in my life; there are many others as well.

On Thursday mornings I used to visit St. Anne's Day Centre to give out pay packets to our three employed members of staff, whilst Ann, a lady from the Alzheimer's Society, used to keep company with Audrey. This is what happened recently. On the way I passed Richard, a young friend of mine, who was on foot. He was out of his territory by about a mile so I offered him a lift. He was on his way home from the car exhaust fitters. The thought came to me that he might be interested in seeing the inside of St. Anne's Day Centre and learn what I got up to in my spare time. His father Sam, a great friend of ours, died several years ago. Shortly after this, his mother Elizabeth was knocked down by a woman driver high on drugs who had jumped the traffic lights. Her legs were shattered, her pelvis was broken and one lung punctured. Elizabeth lay in a coma for several weeks. Three years on she has regained her spirit but is now wheel-chair bound. Richard, a barrister, gave up work to look after her. Recently she invited me around for lunch whilst Richard did a Jamie Oliver act cooking! We had a wonderful talk for nearly three hours. Richard was most impressed by the work that goes on at St. Anne's Day Centre where about fifty homeless people drop-in daily for help with their troubles and for a breakfast and lunch meal. Immediately he was au fait with the problems they have and difficulties they suffer representing their cases to Authority. "I can help them with legal work as I know the ins and outs of all this nonsense; I would enjoy having something useful to do" or words to that effect. "Would you be prepared to serve on our committee," said I. "Yes" he answered. I was able to drive him back to the exhaust fitters thus saving him a mile long walk in the hot sun! In fact he started to run a free weekly legal surgery for our homeless visitors. This is how you will find Divine Providence works time and time again. The finger of God can be seen in all such occurrences by those given light. These are not random chances of life; they are engineered sometimes, as in this case, to a window of two or three seconds on the right day! One's spirit leaps for joy when you experience one of these happenings knowing that God is at your side helping you to do His will.

Divine Providence was there for me when I came to 'The fork in the road' back in 1967 and gave me guidance like this. Then the Army no longer required my services after twenty-three years due to a forces reduction. What to do? I hadn't a clue. My younger brother David's former teacher, Eric North, had emigrated to Australia at the end of war and had just returned to the UK to bury his mother. He was a great friend of my mother's during the War Years of the 1940s and got my address from her. He visited me for a couple of hours before returning home. "Why don't you go into teaching," he suggested, "I know an ex-army major who has done so and will ask him to write to you with advice." This was a new career I had not even thought of. Eric's idea caught on. I took this heaven sent life-line and after two years training became the woodwork teacher at St.

John's RC School in Gravesend. I was really happy to follow in the footsteps of the Divine Son of Joseph, the carpenter, working with wood and helping children. Academics tend to look down on practical teachers but teaching and learning the work of human hands gives joy both to the teacher and pupils and helps to develop their whole personalities. Deo Gratias for Eric North the messenger of Divine Providence from afar! Do not dismiss such occurrences and say "It's just another coincidence" like other sceptics.

Here is a Late Night Final report on Providence! Pippa Kearon's cover picture, which adorns my book, came together by Divine Providence — just like this. Recently I had to visit Mike and Heather Kearon on St. Anne's Day Centre business. Heather chanced to show me a greetings card from their daughter. Their card was faced with Pippa's glorious sunset picture taken at West Cove Pier, Caherdaniel, County Kerry, Ireland — Deo Gratias!

Divine Providence gave me a nudge, the time and talents to write this book. All our talents are given from above. They are not of our own making. Should you believe this book has been inspired by the Holy Spirit for your benefit dear reader, perhaps another person will learn to trust in Divine Providence.

Prayer will help solve the problems of carers, those with a loss of faith, those who have lost their way or suffer ill-health and other of life's problems. It is the panacea for all ills! If you find that prayer works, thank God for the graces He gives you in reply and you will be given even more. The more you trust God, the greater is His response. Be ready to see the hand of God at work in your life so proving He loves you.

Ask - and it will be given to you.

(Matthew 7:7)

32

The Mystery of Light

The Word was the true light that enlightens all men.

(John 1:9)

Light is wonderful and complex stuff somehow made up of the colours of the rainbow. It reflects and refracts and does many other marvellous tricks which are beyond the scope of this book but not to the physicist studying Light. For believers in a deity, light was created by God. As given in Genesis (1:3) it happened like this: And God said, "Let there be light," and there was light. And as one comic put it "And you could see for miles and miles and miles." This sort of light can be seen with our eyes and sadly, those who are blind are deprived of this faculty.

Let us call this "Physical Light."

An equally wonderful light is that of being able to "see" with the mind. "I'm beginning to see the light" as the song goes; and "I see what you mean" or "The penny has dropped." Understanding and Comprehension are the psychological terms for seeing with the mind. Numerous educational disciplines help us to improve our mental capacity. Happily most blind people are sharper mentally in their specific areas of knowledge than are the sighted. Sadly those who suffer dementia in one of its many forms are slowly but surely deprived of this faculty.

Let us call this "Mental Light."

The most wonderful light of all is to understand and to know somewhere within one's being that there is a God and that there is such a state of being as eternal life which we enter into at death. To see this light more clearly one has to resort to prayer. Pope John Paul II had a very busy job but is said to have prayed for seven to eight hours daily. Sadly atheists and agnostics are deprived or deprive themselves of this faculty. The 'wisdom' they claim to have knows better than to suppose that creation had a creator. A lack of prayer will blunt spiritual vision. Of all three forms it is the most mysterious.

Let us call this "Spiritual Light."

Very different from those who suffer the loss of their sight or from those who are spiritually blind is the situation of those who gradually suffer the loss of their mental faculties due to dementia: their situation requires special comment. These poor people appear to experience a state of worsening spiritual vision since this depends on our mental faculties and our ability to pray. My thoughts on some important moral factors of the matter follow.

My reason tells me that this Spiritual Light is put there by God the Creator of life as a spark of Living Light into every new human being at the moment of conception. This Light is in effect our immortal soul that never dies and cannot go out. For those born into a Christian family, this Light should be nurtured after birth by parents during the child's early life. For children who suffer mental disabilities that deprive them of the mental ability to accept spiritual concepts, then their parents or carers have a spiritual duty to guard this Light for them (how, or why this spark of Light develops into a beam of Light for others not of the Christian faith, seems to me to be a random gift of the Holy Spirit! But, I am equally sure it wouldn't be random!!) As the parents' Christian duty is to nurture the beliefs of their infants onwards as mental capacity advances, my belief is that the well carer of those whose mental faculties are slowly snuffed out by health problems, such as dementia, has the same Christian duty in the reverse direction. The practice of passing a partner so afflicted to outside agencies prematurely simply for convenience, rather than for the health of both partners, is unloving. Pray fervently for them and it is certain the Lord will keep them in His care for you. If you look too far ahead, which is the way of the worldly wise, you start to drown from the enormity of the problem. "Live one day at a time" is one of the maxims of Christ our Saviour which is sound advice as none of us know the day or the hour.

The Mystery of Light – St. John, an old man in his 86th year, the disciple that Jesus loved, had known the Light of the World in His human garb of the flesh. John, with Peter and James had, for a brief moment, met Him in His heavenly body on Mount Tabor at the Transfiguration. After many years of pondering on the events of his life, he is inspired to set down on paper his exposition of this Mystery of Light which is beyond human understanding. He sits down at a table, surely a wooden one, perhaps made by his Divine Master as a teenager in the carpenter's shop at Nazareth for His Mother as a birthday present and left behind in St. John's home when she was assumed into heaven. — God the Creator of the universe makes a table! He starts writing and the most beautiful and spiritually revealing words of all the four gospels flow from his pen about the Mystery of Light.

In the beginning was the Word: the Word was with God, and the Word was God. He was with God in the beginning.

Through Him all things came to be, not one thing had its being but through Him. All that came to be had life in Him and that life was the light of men, a light that shines in the dark, a light that darkness could not overpower.

A man came, sent by God. His name was John. He came as a witness, as a witness to speak for the light, so that everyone might believe through Him. He was not the light, only a witness to speak for the light.

The Word was the true light that enlightens all men; and He was coming into the world. He was in the world that had its being through Him, and the world did not know Him. He came to His own domain and His own people did not accept Him. But to all who did accept Him He gave power to become the children of God, to all who believe in the name of Him who are born not out of human stock or urge of the flesh or will of man but of God himself.

The Word was made flesh, He lived among us, and we saw His glory, the glory that is His as the only Son of the Father, full of grace and truth.

(John 1:1-14)

The spread of this Spiritual Light after the death, and resurrection of Our Lord lay fallow for fifty days until Pentecost Sunday. There is an explanation in the Mass readings of this day of how the rays of this Light began and continue to shine out everywhere. These readings follow because there is no substitute for them.

In the First Reading we learn that the Holy Spirit gave the gift of tongues to the Apostles so that their listeners could hear them tell of the marvels of God in their own native language which is a very sound argument for use of the vernacular in the worship and praise of God. Please don't skip them although you may perhaps know them well already. Like a much loved piece of music that can be played countless times without losing its appeal, a reading of real substance will become more eloquent and spiritually significant with repetition. Thus, some of this Spiritual Light we are discussing enters the soul more deeply like rain dropping softly. A number of well known prayers like the Our Father and Hail Mary said devoutly rather than gabbled give a similar reward.

FIRST READING (Acts 2:1-11)

When Pentecost day came round, the apostles had all met in one room, when suddenly they heard what sounded like a powerful wind from heaven, the noise of which filled the entire house in which they were sitting; and something appeared to them that seemed like tongues of fire; these separated and came to rest on the head of each of them. They were all filled with the Holy Spirit, and began to speak foreign languages as the Spirit gave them the gift of speech.

Now there were devout men living in Jerusalem from every nation under heaven, and at this sound they all assembled, each one bewildered to hear these men speaking in his own language. They were amazed and astonished. "Surely," they said, "all these men speaking are Galileans? How does it happen that each of us hears them in his own native language? Parthians, Medes and Elamites; people from Mesopotamia, Judea and Cappadocia, Pontus and Asia, Phrygia and Pamphylia, Egypt and the parts of Libya round Cyrene; as well as visitors from Rome — Jews and proselytes alike — Cretans and Arabs; we hear them preaching in our own language about the marvels of God."

SECOND READING (1 Corinthians 12:3-7, 12-13)

No one can say, "Jesus is Lord" unless he is under the influence of the Holy Spirit. There is a variety of gifts but always the same spirit; there are all sorts of service to be done, but always to the same Lord; working in all sorts of different ways in different people, it is the same God who is working in all of them. The particular way in which the Spirit is given to each person is for a good purpose.

Just as a human body, though it is made up of many parts, is a single unit because all these parts, though many, make one body, so it is with Christ. In the one Spirit we were all baptised, Jews as well as Greeks, slaves as well as citizens, and one Spirit was given to us all to drink.

THE GOSPEL (John 20:19-23)

In the evening of that same day, the first day of the week, the door was closed in the room where the disciples were for fear of the Jews. Jesus came and stood among them. He said to them, "Peace be to you," and showed them His hands and His side. The disciples were filled with joy when they saw the Lord, and He said to them again, "Peace be to you. As the Father has sent me, so am I sending you." And saying this He breathed on them and said: "Receive the Holy Spirit, for those whose sins you forgive, they are forgiven, for those whose sins you retain, they are retained."

Spiritual Light is a Mystery

Whilst the finite human mind cannot fathom the infinite mystery of Spiritual Light, by listening to the Word of God, true light will enlighten your soul. We have the following promise –

"I am the Light of the World. So if you follow me, you won't be stumbling through the darkness, for living Light will flood your path." (John 8:12)

Our Lord's journey through His life on earth, recorded in the New Testament, tells us of the route He took for us to follow, culminating with The Way of the Cross. The closer we get to Him, the easier He is to follow. You get close to a person by conversing with them. In the gospels there are numerous examples of Our Lord going away alone to pray to His heavenly Father. "So if you follow me . . . . !"

Walk in the light. . . . .

(John 12:35)

Channels of Spiritual Light

To receive the enlightenment of Spiritual Light one must resort to prayer which is defined as 'The raising of the mind and heart to God.' Generalising, prayer can take three principal forms –

Prayer from the Heart

A book by Sister Emmanuel on Medjugorje *Triumph of the Heart* gives a wonderful example of 'Prayer from the Heart.' This is prefaced by Our Lady's message to the children of Medjugorje dated 25th April 1991. This was as follows –

"Dear children! Today I invite you all so that your prayer be prayer from the heart. Let each one of you find time for prayer so that in prayer you discover God. I do not desire you to talk about prayer, but to pray. Let each of your days be filled with gratitude to God for life and all that you have. I do not desire your life to pass by in words but that you glorify God with deeds. I am with you and I am grateful to God for every moment spent with you. Thank you for having responded to my call."

Pilgrims, even today, often ask how to 'pray from the heart.' They are very relieved to learn, after their experience of Medjugorje's great simplicity, that they had already known it but were not aware of it.

They arrive with intellectual concerns, but go back home with the solid good sense of children, of little ones, those to whom the mysteries of the Kingdom are revealed.

IT'S ME, PAUL!

A French priest gave us a marvellous illustration of 'prayer from the heart' one day in church by relating a trivial event which took place in Paris:

Paul spent most of his time in the open. So he really appreciated St. Jacques Church porch, where he used to beg. To be honest, we must add a bottle of wine was keeping him company. Amongst his many illnesses, he suffered from cirrhosis of the liver — another faithful companion of his. You could tell by the colour of his face. People in the neighbourhood expected him to disappear sooner than later. However, nobody was really interested in him.

Still, a good-hearted lady of the parish, Mrs. N., had initiated a kind of dialogue with him. The terrible loneliness of this man saddened her. She had also noticed that, in the morning, he would temporarily leave his spot in the porch, go into the church — as empty as ever — sit on a pew in the front row, and face the tabernacle. He would sit there and do nothing.

One day she said to him, "Paul, I've seen you walk into the church many times. But what do you do while sitting there? You have no rosary, no prayer book, you even at times doze a little … What do you do over there? Do you pray?"

"How could I possibly pray? I can't even remember a word of the prayers I was taught at Sunday school when I was a kid! I have forgotten everything! What do I do? It's simple! I go to the tabernacle where Jesus is alone in his little box, and I tell him: 'Jesus! It's me, Paul! I've come to see you' and I sit there for a while just to show I'm around!'"

Mrs. N. was speechless. She never forgot what he said. Days came and went as usual. Then one day, what was bound to happen, happened. Paul disappeared from the porch. Was he sick? Dead, maybe? Mrs N. decided to find out and finally located him in a hospital. She visited him. Poor Paul. He was a dreadful sight! he was covered with tubing and his complexion was grey and pasty. He looked like someone who was about to die. In addition the medical prognosis was less than optimistic.

She returned the next day expecting to hear bad news, but no, Paul was sitting bolt upright in his bed, clean-shaven, looking fresh and completely changed! An expression of immeasurable joy emanated from his face. He looked radiant. Mrs. N. rubbed her eyes. Without a doubt, it was he!

"Paul! This is unbelievable. You're resurrected! You are not the same person anymore. What on earth happened to you?"

"Well, it all happened this morning. I wasn't too well, you know, and suddenly I saw someone coming in and standing at the foot of my bed. He was so handsome, so handsome. ... You can't even imagine! He smiled at me and said,"

"Paul! It is I, Jesus! I've come to see you!"

I thought I had finished at this point and went back to bed, but my inner voice told me … 'No — something more needs to said about this incident — have a go and see what comes out.'

Long ago St. Paul had a meeting with Jesus as the 'Source of All Light' on the road to Damascus with shattering effects. Quite recently in Paris, our second Paul had an infinitely more gentle and heart-tugging experience in meeting Jesus. It brings tears to the eyes of many, including myself, when they read of it.

Paul's habit of dropping-in to keep Jesus company is the work of a Good Samaritan. However, once in the presence of Our Lord doubtless he was contrite for his faults and failings. So as Good Samaritan and Prodigal Son he is accorded the most gentle and loving meeting with his and our Saviour. We also meet another Good Samaritan in Mrs N. Her reward was to see Paul after his instant cure and to share in Paul's supreme joy at meeting Jesus in person. Somehow, we readers also feel his joy. Expect sceptics to argue that Paul hallucinated; and was cured?! Jesus has given us Paul (a most unlikely model) as an example to follow — or shame on us all. What about a resolution?

"Dear Lord and Father of Mankind, I resolve to keep You company in Your little box more frequently from this day on." If more of us did so, then there would be no need for churches to be locked during the day with Jesus imprisoned in solitary confinement.

In St. Luke's gospel (Luke 4:22) Luke tells us –

". . . . and all were amazed by the gracious words that came from His lips." Now, in our own times, from just one example of a few simple words from His lips, one is struck immediately by Our Lord's perfect grammar — "Paul! It is I, Jesus!" He gives Paul a gentle lesson and us too. St Luke chose the phrase 'Gracious Words' and meant it in every sense.

Of course! — Words from the Word of God preaching in Galilee would be perfect — no slovenly speech would have come from His lips. His verbal charisma lay in the perfection of content, form and cadence. It was an amazing joy to hear Him speak.

Jesus has said "Follow me!" As the Word of God, let us follow Him in all He does and says. Imagine how pleasant and peaceful life would be if we copied His example in speech — no belligerence, profanity, raised voices and we allowed nothing nasty ever to pass our lips — even to the point of perfection in trying not to corrupt our own mother tongue whatever it be. (cf. prayer LIKE CHRIST p.77)

Oh that our tongues might so possess
The accents of His gentleness.
. . . .
Oh that it might be said of us,
"Surely thy speech betrayeth thee
As friends of Christ of Galilee."

42

Prayer from the Hands

Our Lord, the Creator, sanctified the honest work of human hands by His days in the Carpenter's shop at Nazareth. The monks and nuns of old (and even of today) had time set aside each day for the 'work of human hands,' farming, gardening, manuscript writing, building abbey churches, cooking and feeding the poor, caring for the sick and so on.

God the Creator guides all those who undertake creative work with sincerity. This is another way in which Divine Providence takes a hand in our lives. We all experience the joy of wonderment when our work turns out infinitely better than expected. But, don't get proud and pat yourself on the back — rather stand back and admire God's work through your hands and say — Deo Gratias!

To sanctify our daily work, all that is necessary is to make a morning offering on rising each day, such as –

O Dear and loving Lord, I offer you the prayers, works, deeds and actions of this day for all the intentions of thy most Sacred Heart – Amen.

In fact at every Mass during the offertory, the words of the celebrant recognise our offering is made possible by a most important 'Prayer from the Hands' by saying –

Blessed are you, Lord, God of all creation. Through your goodness we have this bread to offer, which earth has given and human hands have made. It will become for us the bread of life.

Blessed be God forever.

Blessed are you Lord, God of all creation. Through your goodness we have this wine to offer, fruit of the vine and work of human hands. It will become our spiritual drink.

Blessed be God forever.

Prayer from the Mind, Heart and Lips.

Such prayers are dealt with in the next four parts. However, I include a few words of introduction on each of these.

The Rosary Way – The first part is about the Holy Rosary and how to say it and gives some comments about this prayer. Pope John Paul II recommended saying the Rosary daily for World Peace. He had a very great devotion to Our Lady of Fatima and in this he was simply echoing her requests. Many people carry a set of rosary beads in their pocket or purse.

A Gloria of Prayers – This is followed by a section devoted to some popular formal set prayers and other spiritual thoughts that may appeal. It contains a two page section of prayers for children. Several of these can be learnt by heart to use and to cherish for the rest of their lives.

The Way of the Cross – We follow our Lord up the 'Via Dolorosa' to Calvary. This is a little pilgrimage of prayer as one moves from station to station. It is a most neglected prayer that only comes into prominence during Lent. But there are those who say it at other times. They have their own shortened form which consists of a genuflection at each station, a gaze at the 'work of art' and just a few words such as "We adore thee O Christ and praise thee because by thy Holy Cross Thou has redeemed the world." The form presented here can be learnt off by heart.

The Way to God – Here we talk of searching for and finding God. There are thoughts from Cardinal Basil Hume and St. Bernard on the use of solitude and time for loving God and serving others in our quest. The prayer of Fr. Bede Jarratt "The Abiding City" tells us how to follow Our Lord and so reach our eternal destination in Him.

Earlier we read of Paul raising his mind and heart to God in silent prayer before the tabernacle. Our Lady invited the children of Medjugorje to "Pray from the heart so that they discovered God." Cardinal Basil Hume in his book *Searching for God* talks of a similar type of prayer he calls 'The Prayer of Quiet' and describes its form like this:-

"This prayer, whether it be for five minutes or half an hour, dispenses with words, images and ideas. Yet that does not mean that these have to be totally excluded. What matters is that we have to be totally silent in the presence of God: that we cultivate a silent awareness in which the soul meets God deep within itself."

P.S. (You will like this one!)

A visit to see 'Jesus in His little box' to tell Him you are about is a beautiful "Prayer of Quiet" from the heart where your soul can meet God. Whilst you are in church why not light a votive candle to the 'Light of the World' in petition for those you wish to pray for and others who are most in need of prayer.

My Prayer on Lighting a Candle. Lord may this candle be a light for You to enlighten me in my difficulties and decisions. May it be a fire for You to burn out of me all pride, selfishness and impurity. May it be a flame for You to bring warmth into my heart towards my family, neighbours and all those who meet me. Through the prayer of Mary Virgin and Mother I place in Your care those I came to remember especially (. . . . .). I cannot stay long with You in Your church. In leaving this candle I wish to give You something of myself. Help me to continue my prayer into everything I do this day. Amen.

"Let us do Something Beautiful for God."

(Blessed Teresa)

45

THE

ROSARY

WAY

Hail Full of Grace!

"Hail, thou who art full of grace; the Lord is with thee; blessed art thou among women …" and Mary answered — "Behold the handmaid of the Lord; let it be unto me according to thy word." (Luke 1:28)

The Rosary is a contemplative prayer of twenty mysteries offered in petition to Mary, The Mother of God. The first Mystery of the Rosary 'The Annunciation' starts with the Archangel Gabriel's salutation to Mary given above. Her response was her Song of Joy. Mary begins with praise of God as all true prayer should. Next is her expression of spiritual joy on learning that she is to be the instrument of salvation; then humility and finally prophecy.

Mary's Song of Joy

My soul glorifies the Lord;
My spirit has found joy in God my Saviour,
Because He looked graciously upon the
Lowliness of His handmaid
From now on all generations will call me blessed
For the Almighty has done great things for me,
And holy is His Name.
(Luke 1:46-49)

The Curé D'Ars, St. John Vianney, said these words of Our Lady and the Rosary –

"Although Mary knew that God had raised her to the most supreme of all honours — that of being the Mother of God — nevertheless she regarded herself as the least of all creatures."

"It is impossible to meditate with devotion upon the Mysteries of the Rosary and live in a state of sin."

"We ought to love the Blessed Virgin very much."

Our Father
Fatima Prayer
Glory Be

Ten
Hail
Marys

Our Father   Glory be

Three
Hail
Marys

Our Father

The
Apostles'
Creed

"The Blessed Virgin's life was full of sorrow… Every time her tender glance fell upon her Divine Son, she suffered… "

The depth of Mary's anguish on The Via Dolorosa and on Calvary by the foot of the Cross is beyond our imagination. She shared in Our Lord's sufferings for us. From the cross His words to her were "Woman, behold your son," and to John "Son, behold your mother." So it is true we ought to love her very much and she loves us as her children in the risen Christ.

Tradition has it, but it is not recorded in the Gospels, that after His resurrection Jesus showed himself first to His Blessed Mother.

The Rosary, consisting as it does of 'The Apostles' Creed,' Our Lord's prayer 'The Our Father,' the Archangel Gabriel's salutation to Mary 'The Hail Mary …' and 'The Glory Be' — the prayer of praise to the Trinity, makes it perhaps the second greatest prayer of all, second to the Mass. Only a priest can say a Mass, but all of us can say the Rosary any time, any place by ourselves. If you say it in company, remember Our Lord's words —
"When two or three of you are met together in my name, there am I in the midst of you." (Matt. 18:20)

And never forget the prayer that will always be answered — "Holy Mary, Mother of God, pray for us sinners now and at the hour of our death. Amen"

In 1917, near Fatima in Portugal, Our Blessed Lady appeared to three shepherd children on six successive months. One of her requests to them was that they should pray the Rosary daily for World Peace and asked them to say her Fatima Prayer after each decade.

The picture opposite shows the author's pocket Rosary said to be made in Bethlehem of olive-wood beads. The prayer sequence shown is discussed in detail later.

The Rosary as a Prayer

A Rosary is an essential aid for praying the Rosary. The use of one's fingers as beads just doesn't work! Passing the beads through one's fingers, forming the words silently with the lips (or aloud in company) and in contemplating each mystery the while, means that this prayer is thereby given both a human and spiritual depth. I believe that Rosary beads that are used are sanctified by their use. When I am up and about during the day having them in my pocket is a most important part of my persona Thereby one in never alone – the Queen of the most Holy Rosary is with you.

Many persons find praying the Rosary very hard work. So hard in fact they strike it off their list of prayers. Others sheepishly say they find it boring (The Good Shepherd perhaps will find a way to lead them to appreciate its efficacy). The author admits to having been one such person for most of his life until one night three years ago I was in desperate straits for some form of diversion from the stresses I was under at the time. Praying the Rosary solved my stresses and has done so ever since. In fact said last thing at night it is very likely to help you to drop off to sleep but we do not say it for that reason do we?! If said lying down all cosy in bed, you may find you drop off before its completion which is a discourtesy to avoid if you know that it is likely to happen! The answer is to sit on the bed or kneel beside it. Then on lying down an Our Father, Hail Mary and Glory Be and the Fatima prayer sets one up for a personal talk with Our Lord to thank him for the Graces you have received during the day and you will go to sleep at peace.

In the 'Gloria of Prayers' part is a prayer titled 'Slow me down.' Its last lines read — 'Slow me down, Lord! Inspire me to send my roots deep into the soil of life's enduring values.' Saying the Rosary habitually does exactly that. It forms a firm base of a prayer life and moreover it leads to a tendency to pray more often.

I get a lot of pleasure offering up the Rosary for many of my friends and acquaintances who are sick, have monumental worries and also those who have died for 'It is a holy and wholesome thought to pray for the dead that they may be loosed from their sins.' In fact I feel I've made many friends for eternity that I haven't yet met in person. Usually, the parish newsletter asks for prayers for those who have died during the week and some of these get several rosaries said for them when I've no other person on my prayer list. However, this is usually quite full because my friends flatter me by asking me to pray for their intentions.

St. Paul tells of the athletes who punish themselves to win a cup or a crown just to put on a shelf to look at and to be thought well of. Such worthless baubles require terrible graft to earn and you cannot take them with you. Egotistical pursuits do not have the same sanctifying value as prayer and good works which help share Divine Providence with others and will store up treasures in heaven.

The Rosary said devoutly takes some twenty minutes to say which only takes a small amount of commitment and effort. But, you are only giving a little bit back to God of the day you have been given by him. It is a prayer that is answered immediately in that it brings solace to all and most especially to those who live alone and maybe are sick or suffering in one way or another. Invariably, despite the fact you may have a heavy cross to bear, something during the day may well have gone well that you can thank God for. Blessed Teresa of Calcutta suggested you thanked God for the crosses you are given because it means He loves you!

About the Rosary

In earlier times the Rosary was a prayer necklace of fifteen sets of ten beads called a decade. Each decade covered one of fifteen episodes, termed mysteries, in the lives of Jesus and Mary. These were in groups of five Joyful, Sorrowful and Glorious mysteries. The five Joyful Mysteries relate to the lives of Mary and Jesus until His age was twelve. The Sorrowful cover His passion and death on the cross and the Glorious mysteries start with His resurrection from the dead.

In October 2002 Pope John Paul II added another set of Mysteries called 'The Mysteries of Light' to the Rosary so increasing the number of decades to twenty. Living Light had revealed to his Holiness that the whole Rosary was an incomplete meditation on Jesus' and Mary's life. On reflection, all can now see that there was no provision in the Rosary for meditating upon the mysteries revealed during Our Lord's public life which showed Him to be truly the Son of God. Five principal rays of Light from His public life are chosen for meditation. Why had it taken so long for this prayer to come to perfection? We have it in the words of St. Peter "With the Lord a day is like a thousand years, and a thousand years are like a day" (2 Peter 3:8). With the completion of the four sets of mysteries, Pope John Paul II by the Light of the Holy Spirit had, in human parlance, dealt us four aces!

The Rosary is now a rounded meditation on the story of the New Testament. Through the beads we follow the lives of Mary and Jesus. We follow Mary from the day the Archangel Gabriel told her she was to become the Mother of Christ, to the day she was crowned Queen of Heaven. We follow Jesus from the moment the Holy Spirit came down on Mary, through His childhood, His public life, His cruel death on the Cross, the joy of

Easter when He rose from the dead, to the day He ascended to Heaven in Glory.

These four sets of mysteries can also be seen to reflect our own life stories as we follow Our Lord — We are born (Joyful); we live a life (Light); suffer and die (Sorrowful); are given life everlasting (Glorious).

Each set of five decades is now held to be a Rosary and a set of rosary beads is made for saying these.

Mary waits for your prayers. If you speak to her she always listens. She is our mother. When you pray the Rosary, begin by telling Mary what you would like her to use your prayers for — then think about the stories relating to each decade as you say it. When John Paul II added the Mysteries of Light to the whole Rosary he called us to pray the Rosary daily; for our families and for world peace. In addition to this dedication, offer the Rosary for any number of other intentions you wish — Heaven is the limit.

For those who pray a Rosary daily by oneself or in a group, it is customary to match sets of mysteries to the appropriate day of the week.

Monday and Saturday	- - - - - - -	Joyful
Tuesday and Friday	- - - - - -	Sorrowful
Wednesday and Sunday	- - - - -	Glorious
Thursday	- - - - - - - - - - - - - -	Light

The Joyful are said on Sundays during Advent.

And the Sorrowful are said on the Sundays in Lent.

The Joyful Mysteries

These relate to the Incarnation of God the Son in the person of Jesus and cover five principal mysteries in His life from His conception until the time He began His public life at the age of thirty. From being lost and found in the Temple at the age of twelve, we only know that — "He went down to Nazareth and was obedient to them and grew in wisdom and stature, and in favour with God and Men" (Luke 2:51-52).

1. The Annunciation. "When the angel had come to her he said, "Hail, full of grace, the Lord is with thee. Blessed art thou among women." (Luke 1:28)

2. The Visitation. "And Elizabeth was filled with the Holy Spirit, and cried out "Blessed art thou among women and blessed is the fruit of thy womb!" (Luke 1:41-42)

3. The Birth of Jesus. "And she brought forth her firstborn son, and wrapped Him in swaddling clothes, and laid Him in a manger because there was no room for them at the inn." (Luke 2:7)

4. The Presentation. "And when the days of her purification were fulfilled according to the Law of Moses, they took Him up to Jerusalem to present Him to the Lord." (Luke 2:22-23)

5. Finding of the Child Jesus in the Temple. "And it came to pass after three days, that they found Him in the temple, sitting in the midst of teachers, both listening to them and asking them questions." (Luke 2:46)

The Mysteries of Light

These relate to events in the public life of Jesus and may be seen as flashes of The Divine Light of inspiration given to us to help us sanctify our lives "Be ye holy as your heavenly Father is Holy." In these mysteries the Divinity of Christ is shown to us so that we can follow Jesus on our way in life with assurance.

1. Christ's Baptism in the Jordan. "The Spirit descended like a dove on Him, and a voice came from heaven, 'You are my son, the Beloved; and with You I am well pleased.'" (Mark 1:10).

2. Christ's Self-revelation at the Marriage at Cana. "Jesus changed water into wine, the first of His signs, and revealed His glory; and His disciples believed in Him." (John 2:11)

3. Christ's Proclamation of the Kingdom of God with his Call to conversion. "The time is fulfilled, and the kingdom of God has come near: repent and believe in the good news." (Mark 1:15)

4. Christ's Transfiguration. "And He was transfigured before them, and His face shone like the sun, and His clothes became dazzling white." (Matthew 17:2)

5. Christ's Institution of the Eucharist. "He took bread, broke it and gave it to them saying, 'This is my body which is given for you. Do this in remembrance of me.'" (Luke 22:19)

The Sorrowful Mysteries

From the start of Our Lord's ministry at the age of thirty lasting some three years, the next events in the Rosary cycle of Mysteries follow "The Last Supper." These occur during about eighteen hours before his death on the cross.

1. The Agony in the Garden. "And His sweat became as drops of blood running down upon the ground. And rising from prayer He came to the disciples, and found them asleep, exhausted from sorrow." (Luke 22:44-45)

2. The Scourging at the Pillar. "Pilate, then, took Jesus and had Him scourged." (John 19:1)

3. Crowning with Thorns. "And they stripped Him and put on Him a scarlet cloak, and plaiting a crown of thorns they put it on His Head, and a reed in His right hand." (Matthew 27:28-29)

4. Carrying of the Cross. "And bearing the cross for Himself, He went forth to the place called the skull, in Hebrew, Golgotha." (John 19:17)

5. The Crucifixion. "And Jesus cried out with a loud voice and said 'Father, into thy hand I commend my spirit.' And having said this, He expired." (Luke 23:46)

The Glorious Mysteries

These relate to events which occurred starting on the third day after the crucifixion.

1. The Resurrection. "He is risen, He is not here. Behold the place where they lay Him." (Mark 16:6)

2. The Ascension. "So then the Lord, after He had spoken to them, was taken up into heaven, and sits at the right hand of God." (Mark 16:19)

3. Descent of the Holy Spirit. "And they were all filled with the Holy Spirit and began to speak in foreign tongues. Even as the Holy Spirit prompted them to speak." (Acts 2:4)

4. The Assumption. "And a great sign appeared in heaven: a woman clothed with the sun, and the moon was under her feet, and upon her head a crown of twelve stars." (Apocalypse 12:1)

5. The Coronation. "Thou art the glory of Jerusalem the honour of our people … the hand of the Lord has strengthened thee and therefore thou shall be blessed forever." (Judith 15:9-11)

Comment: The full title of this mystery is "The Coronation of Our Lady as Queen of Heaven and the glory of all the Angels and Saints." We are called at our baptism to be amongst that number.

Comments on the Mysteries of Light

As the subject of this book is "The Way of Light" it seems appropriate to make some comment on these five mysteries only and not on the remaining fifteen.

By meditating on the five Mysteries of Light and on their meaning for us, Spiritual Light dawns brighter and brighter in our souls to lead us nearer to God.

First – At baptism we are baptised "In the name of the Father, Son and Holy Spirit." On joining God's family as His children we are welcomed — "This is my beloved child in whom I am well pleased." As baptised Christians, we are all sons and daughters of God and Jesus tells us to call God "Our Father."

Second – At Cana, Jesus shows Divine Providence by pouring out wine in abundance as a blessing for joy and conviviality. In the same way He shed His precious blood at His passion and death for our everlasting joy.

Third – Conversion, confession and penance are synonyms. Unlike Jesus from the age of twelve to thirty "Who was obedient to his parents and grew in wisdom and stature and in favour with God and Man" (Luke 2:51-52), we indulge in greed and the excesses of the good things of life. Some even make work their god and do not rest on the seventh day. This mystery calls us to be sorry for our sins, to resolve to mend our ways, to believe that Christ has died for our sins and rose again and to "Believe in the Communion of Saints, the forgiveness of sins and life everlasting. Amen."

Fourth – Jesus had three witnesses to the event of His transfiguration, Peter, James and John. Only God knows the future and in foretelling of his resurrection from the dead, this is a further proof for us of the Divinity of Jesus Christ.

St. James does not write about the transfiguration in his epistle, but perhaps his experience at it prompted him to make this definitive statement about the nature of God.

"But whatever is good and perfect comes to us from God, the creator of all light, and He shines for ever without change or shadow."   (James 1:17)

Fifth – Jesus institutes The Most Holy Sacrament at the Last Supper. He is present in the Eucharist and is food for our souls by the mystery of transubstantiation.

Clearly the Holy Spirit inspired Pope John Paul II to add these five Luminous Mysteries to the Holy Rosary.

How to Say the Rosary

The picture on page 50 shows the sequence of prayer going clockwise. A decade starts with an 'Our Father' then ten 'Hail Marys' and a 'Glory Be.' It is usual to say five decades of one of the four sets at a time, but it is better to say one decade well, rather than five decades badly. As you say each decade, think about the linked story in the life of Mary and Jesus. The prayer leader's words, where two of more people say the Rosary, are shown in bold print.

To begin a Rosary make the Sign of the Cross
and say The Sign of the Cross words

In the name of the Father, and of the Son, and of the Holy Spirit. Amen.

Make a dedication such as

I (We) offer this Rosary to the Immaculate Heart of Mary for my family (our families) for world peace and for. .

Name any other specific intentions for which you wish to offer your Rosary. Your Rosary isn't less efficacious if you have a multiple intention. Our Lady is generous!

61

Say the Apostle's Creed holding the crucifix

I believe in God the Father Almighty, Creator of heaven and earth. I believe in Jesus Christ, His only Son, Our Lord. He was conceived by the power of the Holy Spirit and was born of the Virgin Mary. He suffered under Pontius Pilate was crucified, died, and was buried. He descended to the dead. On the third day He rose again. He ascended into heaven, and is seated at the right hand of the Father. He will come again to judge the living and the dead. / I believe in the Holy Spirit, the holy Catholic Church, the Communion of Saints, the forgiveness of sins, the resurrection of the body; and life everlasting. Amen.

Continue on the straight piece of the Rosary of five beads with one Our Father, three Hail Marys which are prayers for the Church. But, most people do not pray these four beads and begin by naming the First Mystery chosen and an Our Father on the fifth bead. So, to start the first decade of the Joyful Mysteries say

The first Joyful Mystery — The Annunciation

Now say one Our Father

Our Father, who art in heaven; hallowed be thy name; Thy kingdom come; Thy will be done on earth as it is in heaven. / Give us this day our daily bread; and forgive us our trespasses as we forgive those who trespass against us, and lead us not into temptation; but deliver us from evil. Amen.

On the circular part of the Rosary say ten Hail Marys

Hail Mary, full of grace, the Lord is with thee; blessed art thou among women, and blessed is the fruit of thy womb, Jesus. / Holy Mary, Mother of God, pray for us sinners, now and at the hour of our death. Amen.

End the first mystery holding the next single bead.

First say a Glory Be

Glory be to the Father, and to the Son, and to the Holy Spirit. / As it was in the beginning, is now, and ever shall be, world without end. Amen.

Then the Fatima Prayer

O my Jesus, forgive us our sins, save us from the fires of hell and lead all souls to heaven especially those who have most need of thy mercy. Amen.

This completes the first mystery.

Start the second mystery on the same single bead and say

The Second Joyful Mystery — The Visitation

Now say an Our Father. Move to the second decade of beads for the next ten Hail Marys. On the next single bead end the second decade by saying a Glory Be and the Fatima Prayer.

Start the third mystery with an Our Father holding that bead. Follow on the decade beads and so on until all five decades have been said. This completes one full circuit of the beads. End the fifth mystery with a Glory Be and the Fatima prayer on the fifth bead of the straight section.

Now say the Hail Holy Queen.

Hail, Holy Queen Mother of Mercy. Hail our life, our sweetness and our hope! To thee do we cry, poor banished children of Eve; to thee do we send up our sighs, mourning and weeping in this vale of tears. Turn then, O most gracious Advocate, thine eyes of mercy towards us and after this our exile show unto us the blessed fruit of thy womb, Jesus; O Clement, O loving, O sweet Virgin Mary. Pray for us, O holy Mother of God, / That we may be made worthy of the promises of Christ.

Let us pray

O God, whose only-begotten son, by his life, death and resurrection has purchased for us the rewards of eternal life; grant we beseech you, that meditating on these mysteries of the most Holy Rosary of the Blessed Virgin Mary, we may both imitate what they contain and obtain what they promise, through the same Christ our Lord. Amen.

May The Divine Assistance remain always with us and may the souls of the faithful departed through the mercy of God Rest in peace. Amen.

The Rosary may end at this point but it is not unusual for the prayer leader to add other prayers for various special intentions. The prayer to St. Michael Archangel is a very powerful extra prayer and is recommended anyway.

Prayer to Saint Michael

Holy Michael, Archangel, defend us in the day of battle; be our safeguard against the wickedness and snares of the devil. May God rebuke him we humbly pray; and do thou Prince of the Heavenly Hosts, by the power of God, thrust down to hell Satan and all other evil spirits who wander through the world for the ruin of souls. Amen.

Finally, make the Sign of the Cross with the words-

In the name of the Father and of the Son and of the Holy Spirit. Amen.

This popular 3rd. Century prayer, associated with saying the Rosary is also often said.

We fly to thy patronage, O Holy Mother of God, Despise not our prayers in our necessities but deliver us from all evils, O glorious and blessed Virgin.

The Litany of the Blessed Virgin Mary

Lord, have mercy. *Lord have mercy*
Christ, have mercy. *Christ have mercy*
Lord, have mercy. *Lord have mercy*
Christ hear us. *Christ graciously hear us*
God the Father of Heaven, *Have mercy on us*
God the Son, Redeemer of the World. *Have mercy on us*
God the Holy Spirit, *Have mercy on us*
Holy Trinity One God *Have mercy on us*
Holy Mary. *Pray for us*
Holy Mother of God "
Holy Virgin of virgins "
Mother of Christ "
Mother of divine grace "
Mother most pure "
Mother most chaste "
Mother inviolate "
Mother most loveable "
Mother most admirable "
Mother of good counsel "
Mother of our Creator "
Mother of our Saviour "
Virgin most prudent "
Virgin most venerable "
Virgin most renowned "
Virgin most powerful "
Virgin most merciful "
Virgin most faithful "

Mirror of Justice. *Pray for us*
Seat of Wisdom. "
Cause of our joy. "

Spiritual Vessel "
Vessel of honour "
Singular vessel of devotion
Mystical Rose "
Tower of David "
House of gold "
Ark of the covenant "
Gate of heaven "
Morning star "
Health of the sick "
Refuge of sinners "
Comfort of the afflicted "
Queen of Angels "
Queen of Patriarchs "
Queen of Prophets "
Queen of Apostles "
Queen of Martyrs "
Queen of Confessors "
Queen of Virgins "
Queen of all Saints "
Queen conceived "
without original sin
Queen assumed into heaven
Queen of the most Holy Rosary
Queen of Peace "
Queen of the family "

Lamb of God, who takes away the sins of the world, *spare us, O Lord*
Lamb of God who takes away the sins of the world, *graciously hear us O Lord*
Lamb of God who takes away the sins of the world, *have mercy on us*.

Pray for us, O Holy Mother of God.
That we may be made worth of the promises of Christ

Let us Pray
Lord God, give to your people the joy of continual health in mind and body. With the prayers of the Virgin Mary to help us, guide us through the sorrows of this life to eternal happiness in the life to come. Grant this through our Lord Jesus Christ, your Son who lives and reigns with you and the Holy Spirit., one God, for ever and ever. *Amen.*

A

GLORIA

OF

PRAYERS

A Gloria of Prayers

Like the title of this book, a collective noun for the heading of this part to describe a collection of prayers was elusive — a pack (?) or gabble (!) didn't seem right. I went to bed praying for guidance. When I awoke quite early, I had a flash of inspiration with the words 'A Gloria of Prayers" — most appropriate — "Thank You Lord!" Divine Providence was at work again.

Many of these prayers, and some hymn words, have been chosen by friends and relations. The most popular prayer for nearly all of those consulted is Saint Bernard's prayer 'The Memorare' on page 71. My mother taught it to my father whilst they were engaged nearly a century ago so it was his best loved prayer. The reason for the inclusion of some of the prayers is given together as with the case of the 'Adoro Te Devote' overleaf. This is my favourite which I say after receiving Holy Communion.

This was learnt the hard way! Back one frosty morning in 1936, Brother Steve Donovan breezed into his Religious Knowledge lesson saying — "You boys can learn this!" We did. Brother Steve had been a Life Guards bandsman in a former life and could play nine instruments — his favourite was the cello and when playing 'The Swan' sounded just like his star, Pablo Casals — it's a fact! He could have made a fortune with his fine baritone voice but spent a religious life in the worship of God and passing on his musical talents to a generation of boys. Steve was a jovial instrument of Divine Providence — Deo Gratias!

My inner voice has suggested a prayer to say whenever I enter God's House so that I do so with due reverence to Our Lord.

Hidden God devoutly I adore Thee.

Adoro Te Devote

Hidden God devoutly I adore Thee,
Truly present underneath these veils
All my heart subdues itself before Thee
Since all before Thee faints and fails.

Not to sight, taste or touch be credit
Hearing only do we trust secure
I believe for God the Son has said it
Word of Truth that ever shall endure.

On the cross was veiled Thy Godhead splendour
Here Thy manhood lieth hidden too
Unto both alike my faith I render
And as sued the contrite thief I sue.

Though I look not on Thy wounds with Thomas
Thee my Lord and Thee my God I call,
Make me more and more believe Thy promise
Hope in Thee and love Thee over all.

Oh Memorial of my Saviour dying,
Living bread that giveth life to man.
May my soul its life from Thee supplying
Taste Thy sweetness as on earth I can.

Deign O Jesus, Pelican from heaven
Me a sinner in Thy blood to lave,
To a single drop of which is given
All the world from all its sin to save.

Contemplating Lord Thy hidden presence,
Grant me what I thirst for and implore
In the revelation of Thine essence
To behold Thy glory evermore.

Amen, Alleluia.

(St. Thomas Aquinas)

The Memorare

Remember, O most loving Virgin Mary, that never was it known that anyone who fled to your protection, implored your help or sought your intercession, was left unaided. Inspired by this confidence I fly unto you O Virgin of Virgins, my Mother. To you I come, before you I stand sinful and sorrowful. O Mother of the Word Incarnate, despise not my petition (here make a petition) but in Your mercy hear and answer me. Amen.

(St. Bernard)

Radiating God's Love

Dear Lord, help me to spread Thy fragrance everywhere I go. Flood my soul with Thy spirit and life.

Penetrate and possess my whole being so utterly that all my life may only be a radiance of Thine. Shine through me, and be so in me that every soul I come in contact with — may feel Thy presence in my soul.

Let them look up and see no longer me — but only Thee O Lord. Stay with me, and then I shall begin to shine as Thou shinest; so to shine as to be a light to others.

The light O Lord will be all from Thee: none of it will be mine; it will be Thou, shining to others through me.

Let me thus praise Thee in a way Thou dost love best, by shining on those around me. Let me preach Thee without preaching, not by words but by example, by the catching force, the sympathetic influence of what I do, the evident fullness of the love my heart bears to Thee.

Amen.

(Adapted by Blessed Teresa from the Prayer of Cardinal John Henry Newman: see p.74)

Peace begins with a smile!

(Blessed Teresa of Calcutta)

_____

The refectorian at school was a lovely genial man who was the size of an ox named Brother John O'Brien. Every day of his life, come hail or shine, he would give every boy he met the same greeting, with a beaming smile on his face, using their Christian name with these words –

"It's a nice day for the race, Michael"

"What race, Brother?"

"The Human Race, Michael."

You could of course answer "Yes Brother," but it did not dampen his smile. It was only recently that I realised this seeming joke was really a good wish prayer to all he met — A sort of 'God is in heaven and all is well here below.' When I remember to, I trot out the same greeting to my friends and it does make them smile. Peace begins with a smile!

_____

But the good man walks along the ever-brightening light of God's favour; the dawn gives way to morning splendour.

(Proverbs 4:18)

_____

Short Way of the Cross prayer

O Jesus who for love of me
Didst bear Thy Cross to Calvary,
In Thy sweet mercy grant to me
To suffer and to die with Thee.

72

Everything We Do

Lord,
May everything we do this day
Begin with your blessing,
And continue with your help.
May everything we say this day,
Begin with your love
And continue with your grace.
May everything we plan this day
Begin with your inspiration
And continue with your peace.
So that throughout our lives
All that we begin in you
May by you be happily ended,
All that we fail to do
May by you be mercifully mended,
And all that we seek though you
May by you be lovingly attended. Amen

(The Prayer Trust)

Jesus, Jesus stay with me
Oh, how much I long for Thee!
Stay, Thou of my friends the best,
Keep possession of my breast.

O Sacrament most holy, O Sacrament Divine,
All praise and all thanksgiving be every moment Thine.

My Jesus Mercy; Mary Help.

Don't fly through life so fast
You forget to smell the flowers.

Radiating God's Love

Dear Jesus, help me spread Thy fragrance everywhere
Flood my soul with Thy Spirit and Thy life.
Penetrate and possess my whole being so utterly that all of
my life may be only a radiance of Thine.
Shine through me and be so in me that every soul
I come into contact with may feel Thy presence within me.
Let them look up and see no longer me,
But only Jesus

(John Henry Newman)

Saying Yes to God

Dear Lord, teach me to be generous;
Teach me to serve you as you deserve,
To give and not to count the cost,
To fight and not to heed the wounds,
To toil and not to seek for rest
To labour and not to seek reward,
Save that of knowing that I do your will.

(St. Ignatius)

Patrick's favourite – (RIP 10th January 2006)

DO NOT look forward to what
Might happen tomorrow;
The same everlasting Father
Who cares for you today,
Will take care of you tomorrow;
And every day.
Either he will shield you from suffering,
Or he will give you the strength to bear it.
Be at peace then, and put aside
All anxious thoughts and imaginations.

(St. Francis de Sales)

74

Slow me down

Slow me down, Lord! Steady my hurried pace
With a vision of the eternal reach of time
Teach me the art of taking minute vacations
Of slowing down to look at a flower…
To chat with an old friend… or to make a new one
To pat a stray dog…
To watch a spider spin a gossamer web…
To smile at a child…
Or to read a few lines from a good book.
Remind me each day that the race is not always to the swift
That there is more in life than increasing it's speed.
Slow me down, Lord!
Inspire me to send my roots deep into the soil
Of life's enduring values.

(Orin Crain)

_____

The Immaculate Conception

O Mary conceived without sin,
Pray for us who have recourse to thee.

(My mother's favourite prayer)

_____

Peace at Last

O Lord,
Support us all the day long of this life,
Until the shadows lengthen,
And evening comes
And the busy world is hushed,
And the fever of life is over,
And our work is done
Then, in your mercy,
Grant us a safe lodging
And a holy rest
And peace at last.

(John Henry Newman)

Preface

Father, all-powerful and ever-living God,
We do well always and everywhere to give
You thanks through Jesus Christ Our Lord.
In Him, who rose from the dead
Our hope of resurrection dawned
The sadness of death gives way
To the bright promise of immortality
Lord, for your faithful people
Life is changed not ended.
When the body of our earthly dwelling lies in death
We gain an everlasting dwelling in heaven.

(Roman Missal)

————————————————————————————————————

Lead, Kindly Light

Lead, Kindly Light, amid the encircling gloom
　　　　Lead thou me on!
The night is dark, and I am far from home —
　　　　Lead thou me on!
Keep thou my feet, I do not ask to see
　　　　The distant scene — one step enough for me.
I was not ever thus, nor prayed that thou
　　　　Shouldst lead me on;
I loved to choose and see my path, but now
　　　　Lead thou me on!
I loved the garish day, and, spite of fears,
　　　　Pride ruled my will: remember not past years.
So long thy power hath blest me, sure it still
　　　　Will lead me on.
O'er moor and fen, o'er crag and torrent, till
　　　　The night is gone;
And with the morn those angel faces smile
Which I have loved long since, and lost awhile.

(John Henry Newman)

Father Rory Kelly, a man of prayer, passed these on to Audrey and me in the 1980s. He was a curate at St. John the Baptist RC Church in Brighton. The first, he said, was a very powerful prayer in adversity, and very easy to remember!

Prayer to the Holy Trinity

Abba Father,
Send your Holy Spirit,
Come Lord Jesus, set us free.

_____

On the Passing of Time

When I was young and saw the sky
Turn gold as day was dying,
I thought of life as a path of light
And my soul as a swallow flying.
But now I'm older in mind and heart
And have heard the night wind crying,
I know that life is a ladder we mount
Upon Christ's Grace relying.
And by His Grace and Holy Love
Unto His will complying.

_____

Like Christ

Oh that our tongues might so possess
The accents of His gentleness.
That every word we breathe should bless.
For those who mourn, a word of cheer;
A word of hope for those who fear
And love for all men far and near.
Oh that it might be said of us –
"Surely thy speech betrayeth thee –
As friends of Christ of Galilee."

Children's Prayers

Some adults use the prayers they learnt in childhood all their lives. My cousin Monica is especially fond of the first of our prayers. She and her husband Patrick, until his death 10th January 2006, often recited this one together. The Guardian Angel prayer is another one not to cast away foolishly. There is one saying of Our Lord which rings in my ears — "Unless you become as little children, you cannot enter the kingdom of heaven." This means we must have implicit trust in God as do little children when they say their prayers. Pray as innocently and fervently as they do. Prayers learnt as a child and used all one's life will be 'Prayers from the Heart.' One such simple Prayer from the Heart is "Befriend me Holy Spirit" on page 116. It is the perfect prayer for a child to learn and retain "A whole life long" and thereby keep close to God.

An Act of Love

Baby Jesus will you lie
In my arms a little while?
I will hold you tenderly
Look at you and you will smile.
Baby Jesus, God and Man
I will love you all I can.

_____

For Help in Prayer

Reach downward from Thy hidden throne
And take my hands of prayer,
And hold them, hold them in your own
In church and everywhere.
And I will lift them up to Thee
Quite often in the day.
Do Thou each time take hold of me
That I may never stray.   Amen

Prayer to My Guardian Angel

O Angel of God, My guardian dear,
To whom God's love commits me here
Ever this day (night) be at my side,
To light and guard,
To rule and guide. Amen

_____

Morning and Evening Prayer

Dear Jesus,
Please Bless Mummy and Daddy,
Granny and Granddad,
My sister Mary,
My brother John,
My brother David,
And make me a good boy.

Dear Jesus I love you,
Mother Mary I love you,
Saint Joseph I love you,
Dear Angel Guardian
Take care of me today (tonight). Amen

_____

To the Child Jesus

Dear Child Divine,
Sweet Brother mine
Be with me all the day

And when the light
Has turned to night,
Be still with me, I pray

Where 'er I be,
Come thou with me,
And never go away. Amen

Co-workers of Mother Teresa Prayer

MAKE US worthy, Lord, to serve our fellow men throughout the world who live and die in poverty and hunger.

GIVE THEM, through our hands, this day their daily bread, and by our understanding love, give peace and joy.

LORD, make me a channel of Thy peace,
That where there is hatred, I may bring love,
That where there is wrong, I may bring the spirit of forgiveness;
That where there is discord, I may bring harmony;
That where there is error, I may bring truth;
That where there is doubt, I may bring faith;
That where there is despair, I may bring hope;
That where there are shadows; I may bring light;
That where there is sadness, I may bring joy.

LORD, grant that I may seek rather to comfort than to be comforted; to understand than to be understood; to love than to be loved; for it is by forgetting self that one finds; it is by forgiving that one is forgiven; it is by dying that one awakens to eternal life. AMEN

In all things may the most holy, the most just,
And the most lovable Will of God be done, praised,
And exalted above all for ever.

Praised be Jesus Christ, praised for ever more.

Sorrow for Sin

Have mercy on me, O God, in your goodness;
In the greatness of your compassion
Wipe out my offence.
Thoroughly wash me from my guilt
And of my sin cleanse me

(Ps. 51:3, 4)

Praise God

Lord, you are great and greatly to
    Be praised;
Great is your power and your wisdom
    Infinite.
We would praise you without ceasing.
You call us to delight in your praise,
    For you have made us for yourself,
    And our hearts are restless until
    They rest in you
                (St. Augustine)

_____

Glory to God in the Highest

Glory to God in the highest
    And peace to his people on earth.
Lord God, heavenly King,
Almighty God and Father,
    We worship you, we give you thanks,
    We praise you for your glory.
Lord Jesus Christ, only Son of the Father,
Lord God, Lamb of God,
You take away the sin of the world;
    Have mercy on us;
You are seated at the right hand of the Father:
    Receive our prayer.
For You alone are the Holy One,
You alone are the Lord,
You alone are the Most High,
    Jesus Christ,
    With the Holy Spirit
    To the glory of God the Father. Amen

             (Roman Missal)

Patron Saint of Helpless Causes

Whilst Audrey was still working, all her colleagues knew she had a 'Hot Line' to St. Jude, her favourite Saint. Most had little faith or none at all, but when in trouble they would plead with her to pray to "Your St. Jude." We visited St. Jude's shrine in Faversham, Kent and also St. Jude's international shrine in New Orleans. This was lit by about a thousand large votive candles. The locals thought that St. Jude was the preserve of North Americans. Audrey politely told them otherwise! She wrote down prayers she liked. Three of these follow the one to St. Jude.

Prayer to St. Jude

St. Jude, glorious apostle, faithful servant,
Friend and relative of our Lord Jesus.
The Catholic Church invoked you universally as
The Patron Saint of helpless causes.
Pray for me that I may receive the consolations
And the help of heaven in all my sufferings
And that I may bless God with the elect
Throughout eternity.   Amen

The Meaning of Prayer

A breath of prayer in the morning
Means a day of blessing sure;
A breath of prayer in the evening
Means a night of rest secure

A breath of prayer in our weakness
Means a clasp of a mighty hand
A breath of prayer when we're lonely
Means Someone to understand.

A breath of prayer in our sorrows
Means comfort and peace and rest.
A breath of prayer in our doubtings
Assures us the Lord knows best.

A breath of prayer in rejoicing
Gives joy and added delight
For they that remember God's Goodness
Go singing far into the night

There's never a year nor a season
That prayer may not bless every hour
And never a soul need be helpless
When linked with God's infinite power.

Penitence and Forgiveness

Lord Jesus, how can I ever thank you enough for the amazing gift of your forgiveness? As I think back over the years, I recall the many times I have wilfully marred the pattern you had designed for my life. The many times I transgressed your commands; fell short of your expectations, hurt you because I harmed others and broke our relationship. I grieve for ever having offended you, but each time my faltering penitence was answered by the free gift of your forgiveness — restoring me to the joy of your salvation — binding up my sores and healing my wounds.

Unworthy as I am, I am deeply grateful for the memory of a thousand absolutions and for that gift of forgiveness that restores the joy in life.

May all glory, all love and all thanksgiving be to You forever — My merciful Healer and Redeemer Jesus Christ, my Lord and my God. Amen

A Christmas Prayer

Dear Lord, please help the almost endless list
Of relatives and friends which I present,
And see to all their needs and keep them safe,
And fill each heart with peace and sweet content.
With skilful hands mend every broken thing,
Shine up the dreams that sometimes seem to fade,
Strengthen faith and guide the faltering steps
Of all the little creatures you have made.

Dear Lord, bring light to the weary world.
Renew each hope and take into account
The patterns of our not-so-perfect lives,
Forgive our sins whatever the amount.
Turn our thoughts towards things of lasting worth
Show us the folly of a wasted day.
Teach us to come to you … no stone so great
That you cannot remove it from our way

Dear Lord, another Christmas day is ours,
And if you will, another brand New Year,
Walk with us, for how easily we tend
To sometimes wonder what we're doing here.
Our time is NOW, help us to use it well,
Good and gentle Jesus, faithful Friend,
In you all things, and so the night departs,
And Love awaits beyond the journey's end.

_____

Every work of love
Brings a person
Face to face
With God

(Blessed Teresa)

84

Audrey was always one to help others. By Divine Providence perhaps her favourite prayers will still serve someone in need. She would like that.

At an earlier stage of her illness whilst she still knew what was happening to her mind, Audrey slipped a prayer card into another one of my prayer books by Father John Woolley titled *I Am With You* unbeknown to me. I returned to dipping into this prayer book quite recently and came across her card.

Its front picture is a posy of flowers with the words — 'The Gift of Wisdom. He who possesses the gift of wisdom possesses a perfect knowledge of the truth and Truth is God.'

On the Reverse she had written

Please pray

for me XX

Her prayer is being answered as she knew it would. She too believes in Divine Providence. Caring angels of Divine Providence are now taking care of Audrey as you will learn in the part 'The Way to God.'

Dear reader, just remember a simple truth — God is in love with you — trust Him to take care of you.

PS. If this book has started to get you hooked on prayer, treat yourself to Fr John Woolley's book — *I Am With You.* In it you will find Our Lord will tell you personally and in His own words how much He loves you.
(ISBN 1 903816 99 8)

———————————————————————————

The deepest feeling always shows itself in silence.

Prayer of the Friends of St Anne's Trust

Help me Lord to live my life in this world of today
In such a way that when we meet face to face
You'll say to me -

"Come blessed of my Father
Possess the kingdom I prepared for you
Before the world began
For I was hungry and you gave me food
Thirsty and you gave me drink
Naked and you covered me
A stranger and you welcomed me
In prison and you came to me
Sick and you cared for me
For when you did it to the least of those
Who are my brothers and sisters
You did it unto me."

(Matt. 25: 34-40)

A Ladder of Love

LOVE is the origin and source of all good things.
Whoever walks in love can neither stray nor be afraid
Love guides, love protects, love leads to the end.

CHRIST our Lord has set this ladder of love for us
And by it we must climb to heaven. We must keep
A firm hold on love, we must show it to one another
And by our progress in it, we climb to heaven.

(From the Christmas Liturgy)

Sorrow for Sin

Have mercy on me, O God, in your goodness;
In the greatness of your compassion wipe out my offence.

(Ps. 51:1)

Family Prayer

Jesus, Mary and Joseph,
                    I give you my heart and my soul.
Jesus, Mary and Joseph,
                    Assist me in my last agony.
Jesus, Mary and Joseph
                    May I breathe forth my soul
                    In peace into your hands.
Most Sacred Heart of Jesus,
                    Protect our family.

The Meaning of my Life

God has created me to do him some definite service:
He has committed some work to me which He has not
    committed to another.
I have my mission — I may never know it in this life,
    But I shall be told it in the next.
I am a link in a chain, a bond of connections between persons.
He has not created me for naught.
I shall do good.
I shall do His work.
I shall be an angel of peace, a preacher of truth in my own
    place while not intending it — if I do but keep His
    commandments.
Whatever, wherever I am, I can never be thrown away.
If I am in sickness my sickness may serve Him.
He does nothing in vain.
He knows what He is about.
He may take away my friends; He may throw me among
    strangers; He may make me feel desolate, make my spirits
    sink, hide my future from me — still He knows what He is
    about.
Therefore, I will trust Him.

                                    John Henry Newman

The Angelus Domini

This is a most beautiful prayer said to the music of the local church bell — the bell-ringer sounds a triple peal of three rings, then nine bells for the 'Let us Pray.' This calls people to say 'The Angelus' at 6am, midday and 6pm. The custom generally died out in England centuries ago. But at school in the 1930s, a game of cricket would stop for the 6pm Angelus bell. We would doff our caps and pray, led by the umpire!

Audrey and I holidayed five times in Croatia on the Island of Hvar. It was wonderful magic to hear the Franciscan Monastery's 6am Angelus bell sounding across the bay over a mile of limpid water.

The Angelus

The Angel of the Lord declared upon Mary;
And she conceived of the Holy Spirit
Hail Mary etc

Behold the handmaid of the Lord;
Be it done to me according to your word.
Hail Mary etc

And the Word was made flesh;
And dwelt among us
Hail Mary etc

Pray for us, O holy Mother of God.
That we may be made worthy of the promises of Christ

Let us Pray

Pour forth we beseech You, O Lord, Your grace into our hearts, that we, to whom the Incarnation of Christ, Your Son, was made known by the message of an angel, may, by His passion and cross, be brought to the glory of His resurrection, through the same Christ our Lord.   Amen.

Prayer before a Crucifix

Behold, O kind and most sweet Jesus, I cast myself on my knees in thy sight, and with the most fervent desire of my soul, I pray and beseech you that you would impress upon my heart lively sentiments of faith, hope and charity, with a true repentance for my sins, and a firm desire of amendment, whilst with deep affection and grief of soul I ponder within myself and mentally contemplate thy five most precious wounds; having before my eyes that which David spoke in prophecy of you, O good Jesus: 'They have pierced my hands and my feet; they have numbered all my bones.'

The Divine Praises

Blessed be God.
Blessed be His holy Name.
Blessed be Jesus Christ, true God and true Man.
Blessed be the name of Jesus.
Blessed be His most Sacred Heart.
Blessed be His most Precious Blood.
Blessed be Jesus in the most holy Sacrament of the Altar.
Blessed be the Holy Spirit, the Paraclete.
Blessed be the great Mother of God, Mary most holy.
Blessed be her holy and Immaculate Conception.
Blessed be her glorious Assumption.
Blessed be the name of Mary, Virgin and Mother.
Blessed be Saint Joseph, her spouse most chaste.
Blessed be God in His Angels and in His Saints.

For Perseverance

Jesus, I am going away for a time, but I trust not without you. You are with me by your grace. I resolve never to leave you by mortal sin. Although I am so weak I have such hope in you. Give me grace to persevere.   Amen.

Prayer of Spiritual Healing for those who suffer change and bereavement.

Be Still My Soul

Be still, my soul: the Lord is on your side;
bear patiently the cross of grief and pain;
leave to your God to order and provide;
in every change He faithful will remain.
Be still, my soul: your best, your heavenly friend,
through thorny ways, leads to a joyful end.

Be still, my soul: your God will undertake
to guide the future as He has the past.
Your hope, your confidence let nothing shake,
all now mysterious shall be clear at last.
Be still, my soul: the tempests still obey
His voice, who ruled them once on Galilee.

Be still, my soul: the hour is hastening on
when we shall be forever with the Lord,
when disappointment, grief and fear are gone,
sorrow forgotten, love's pure joy restored.
Be still, my soul: when change and tears are past,
all safe and blessed we shall meet at last.

Katharina von Schlegel
tr. Jane L. Borthwick (1813-1897)

_____

. . . Your real life is in heaven with Christ and God.

(Col. 3:3)

The treasured words of divine inspiration given below are taken, with permission, from Father John Woolley's book *I Am With You*. Whilst at prayer during prayer-times, Father John received these words of divine encouragement and guidance from the risen Lord Jesus Christ through His Holy Spirit.

The words selected shows that if we trust in God's love, our prayers will be answered.

The Consolation of Prayer

My child, the ideal preparation for answered prayer is ensuring that your *whole life* increasingly reflects your trust in My love — and My power over all creation.

Seeking the help or the healing of those known to you, do not look for instant or superficial results… know that your prayer releases My healing power and loosens any hold of evil.

Thank Me that the person for whom you pray has been *drawn closer* to Me, and is *receiving*. Thank Me that all your prayers — made with My love and power firmly in your mind — are greatly used. Peace and hope will come to many others through you, as your trust deepens.

What a privilege to know that you are linked with My loving, saving activity among My children!

**Whatever you ask in prayer,
Believe that you have it, and it will be so.**

(Mark 11:24)

THE WAY

OF

THE CROSS

The Way of The Cross

An excellent booklet on this subject titled 'We walk with the Lord on the Way of the Cross' is published by The Prayer Trust. The Prayer Trust is a Registered Charity which seeks to promote prayer for everyone especially through the production of inexpensive prayer books.

(Telephone: 01564 792647) or write to:
The Prayer Trust at Our Lady & St Benedict's
Alcester Road,
HENLEY-IN-ARDEN, B95 6BQ

The Trust gave permission to use their complete text but only the beginning and end prayers are used. It is not possible to do all of it justice here. Their coloured 34-page booklet shows The Via Dolorosa and other scenes of Our Lord's way to Calvary. If interested why not write to the above address for a copy and also find out what else they have to raise your prayer life. A beautiful booklet titled 'An Easter Garden of Prayers' makes a wonderful Easter present.

The following fourteen simple images and words will help you follow Our Lord bearing His cross on His horrific climb up The Via Dolorosa to Calvary, being nailed to the cross and final death and burial. Aim to learn the fourteen station titles by heart so you can say the whole from memory. As you say the title words of each station form your own mental image of that scene from the Passion of Our Lord and Saviour.

We now step back in time to Good Friday 0033 AD to meditate on The Way of the Cross.

Prayer to begin our Way of the Cross

Lord Jesus Christ, we ask you to be with us
in a special way as we now begin this walk with
you, and accompany you on your journey of
Sorrow.

May we draw closer to you as we share the
moments of your Passion.

May we understand more deeply the love with
which you offered yourself so willingly on the
Cross for our sakes.

May we be inspired with a true sorrow for all
our faults and failings.

And may we amend our ways so that we can
follow you more closely in our daily lives, and
show love to those we meet.

Amen.

(The Prayer Trust)

After each station meditation say –

We adore you O Christ and we bless you because by
your Holy Cross you have redeemed the world.

. . . Take up your cross and follow me. (Matt. 17:24)

I Jesus is condemned to death.

After having been scourged and crowned with thorns, Jesus was unjustly condemned by Pilate to die on the Cross.

II Jesus is laden with the Cross.

Jesus, in taking the Cross upon him, offered for us to His Father the death he was to undergo.

III Jesus falls for the first time under the Cross.

Jesus was so weakened that he could scarcely walk. He had to carry his heavy load on his shoulders. The soldiers struck him and thus he fell.

IV Jesus meets his afflicted Mother.

Jesus met his blessed Mother, whose soul was pierced by a sword of anguish at the sight of him, whom she loved so tenderly.

V Simon of Cyrene helps Jesus to carry his Cross.

Jesus' heavy burden was shared by Simon the Cyrenean who was ordered to do so by the soldiers.

VI Veronica wipes the face of Jesus.

Veronica, seeing Jesus so ill-used and his face bathed in sweat and blood, offered him her veil with which he wiped his adorable face.

VII Jesus falls for the second time.

The second fall of Jesus under the Cross renewed the pain of all the wounds of his head and members.

VIII Jesus speaks to the women of Jerusalem.

These women wept with compassion at seeing Jesus in such a pitiable state, streaming with blood as he walked along.

IX Jesus falls the third time.

His weakness was extreme and the cruelty of his executioners very great, who tried to hasten his step when he could scarcely walk.

X Jesus is stripped of his garments.

Jesus is stripped of his garments violently. As the garments adhered to his torn flesh, they dragged them off so roughly that the skin came with them.

XI Jesus is nailed to the Cross.

Jesus, having been placed upon the Cross, extended his arms and offered to his eternal Father the sacrifice of His life for our salvation. These barbarians fastened him with nails to the Cross and allowed him to die in anguish.

XII Jesus dies on the Cross.

Jesus, after three hours agony of the Cross, being consumed with anguish, bowed his head and died.

XIII Jesus is taken down from the Cross.

After Jesus was dead, two of his disciples took him down from
the Cross and placed him in the arms of his afflicted mother.

XIV Jesus is laid in the tomb.

The disciples carried the body of Jesus to bury it, accompanied
by his holy Mother, who laid it in the tomb with her own hands.

Final Prayer; Christ Is Risen!

So slow of heart, says Jesus to the disciples
On the road to Emmaus, so slow of heart!
So slow to believe the prophets,
That it was necessary for the Christ
To suffer all these things
And so enter into His glory.

Suffering you take away our sins,
Dying you do away with our death,
Rising you renew our life,
By your Cross and Resurrection
You have redeemed the world.
Lord Jesus, come in glory!

(The Prayer Trust)

Father Eunan Dooley, a Franciscan missionary in Durban (SA) gave me the image shown of the Franciscans' Icon Cross. Such Icons were used to teach and fortify the faith.

Above the head of Christ in Latin is the inscription "Jesus of Nazareth, King of the Jews." The major witnesses of the Crucifixion are Mary the Mother of Jesus and St. John the Beloved on the left; Mary Magdalene, Mary, mother of James and the Centurion are to the right. Of the smaller figures one is Longinus, the Roman soldier who pierced the side of Jesus with a lance, another is Stephaton who offered Jesus the sponge soaked in vinegar. The six angels at the ends of the crossbar are represented as marvelling over the event of the Crucifixion. Whilst at the top of the cross, we see Jesus clothed in regal garments climbing out of the tomb and welcomed to heaven by ten angels. At the very top of the cross the right hand of God the Father raises Jesus from the dead with a blessing on all that Jesus has done.

THE WAY

TO

GOD

Searching for God

This book is concerned with our journey by the way of prayer to eternal life which is the culmination of the Pilgrim's search for God.

In the Preface we speak of the reward promised by Jesus to the Good Thief for his implicit trust in Jesus. Saint Peter and Saint Paul also tell us the only way to God is by trust in Jesus Christ to save us from our sins.

You love him even though you have never seen him: though not seeing him, you trust him; and even now you are happy with the inexpressible joy that comes from heaven itself.

(1 Peter 1:8.)

But now God has shown us a different way to heaven not by being good enough and trying to keep his laws, but by a new way (though not new, really, for the Scriptures told about it long ago). Now God says he will accept and acquit us and declare us not guilty if we trust Jesus Christ to take away our sins. And we can all be saved in the same way, by coming to Christ, no matter who we are or what we have been like. And now in these days also he can receive sinners in this same way because Jesus took away their sins. But isn't it unfair for God to let criminals go free, and say they are innocent? No, for he does it on the basis of their trust in Jesus.

(Romans 3:21, 22, 26)

To trust a person you have to know them; to know them you have to contact them, speak with them; to know and love God you have to pray to Him.

Returning to my own story, the first signs of Audrey's dementia showed up in little ways some eight years ago and about five years ago this was confirmed by scans. I cared for her as well as I could at home, supported by wonderful friends and family, but finally had to let her go into full time residential nursing care so that she would get the proper attention she needed. My own health was worsening and my premature demise would not help her. Care for her started 19th September 2006 and sleep that night was impossible. The only solace I had was the Rosary said many times. The following night was Wednesday and after saying the Glorious Mysteries another sleepless night threatened. But, I was prompted to read Cardinal Basil Hume's book *Searching for God* as a diversion. Near the beginning of his introduction these words appear:

"The Gospel requires that the Christian should be constantly seeking God. This pre-supposes a desire for silence and solitude in order to discover the reality of God's love for us; but equally the Christian must seek to find Christ in his neighbour and to serve Christ in his neighbour's needs."

It seemed to me a message of Divine Providence. I could see the finger of God in my choice of reading.

My hope, dear reader, is that the words and prayers in this book will help meet your needs along The Way of Light .

Early on in the 1980s we would go up to Westminster at Christmas with Co-workers of Mother Teresa. This was to help with the Cardinal's Party for the so-called down-and-outs or homeless. Once the usual 600 guests had stretched to about 700 and some were up aloft in the Minstrels' Gallery and about thirty or more persons formed a chain to pass plates of Christmas food up the stairs. The Cardinal stood half way up the stairs between Audrey and me helping with this shuttle service. We had been given the privilege of a lifetime and she enjoyed a wonderful conversation with him. Principally he was amazed how they could eat as much as had been piled on the plates!

In a strange way Cardinal Basil was there between us again with his words of wisdom. Divine Providence has finally given Audrey and me silence and solitude apart from each other to seek the reality of God's love for us but not in a way of our choosing. God's ways are not our ways. But, thankfully, these words brought a strange peace to my mind and I could accept God's plan for us and dropped off to sleep quite soon afterwards. The fact that I will have to occupy our flat for the remainder of my life without her but supporting her with prayer whilst searching for God and helping others does make sense of life. It is a cross to bear which promises eternal life. By Divine Providence she has been given a place at Saint George's Retreat at Haywards Heath from 18th October 2006 (St. Luke's Feast Day). This is run by the Augustinian Sisters where she will be under a Christian umbrella of loving care until she mercifully passes into eternal life. Thus our joint and yet individual 'Search for God' will be completed for her.

In my own family circle, many of us have had to share in the long sufferings of their soul mates, children and relatives. All of us turn to our Rosary beads for Divine solace. We are given the consolation that it is a privilege to help bear the suffering of our loved ones. Turning to you dear reader, nearly all of us lose a loved one at some point in our lives, either slowly or swiftly, and then have to suffer the enforced silence and solitude that results from the bereavement. Whilst this loneliness has not come about by our own "desire for silence and solitude in order to discover the reality of God's love for us," patient acceptance of this Cross will bring us the consolation of God's love.

A love which we can then freely share with others and thereby "Serve Christ in our neighbour's needs."

At the beginning of this book, we read of the young-old woman coming to one of the cross roads of life. She listened to Wisdom and took the correct fork. But, Wisdom is one of the gifts of the Holy Spirit and to be given this gift it is necessary to pray. When good fortune seems to turn against you there may be another side to the coin. In reality it may be one of God's greatest blessings for you in disguise. Many such changes, unwillingly suffered in the first instance, often work out for the better. Offer up your problems in prayer to Our Lord last thing at night and next morning your mind set will have changed focus and you will see the problem in a more balanced light.

If you are sad or full of despair, begin by saying Our Lord's Prayer 'The Our Father.' Saying just those two words will bring immediate relief because you have started to share your problem with Almighty God, The Lord and Father of Mankind. The rest of Our Lord's Prayer closing with 'Deliver us from evil' does get answered.

If you cannot find the concentration to say the Rosary, the Our Father, Hail Mary and Glory Be said over and over gives worship to God and also brings consolation in times of need. Saying the Fatima prayer too is beneficial as this is a prayer of contrition for sin and for others. Do you remember it?!

"O my Jesus forgive us our sins, save us from the fires of hell and lead all souls to heaven especially those most in need of thy mercy."

If prayer for you is difficult or nearly impossible and your Way to God an uncertainty in your mind and soul, all of us know of two very simple prayers from the heart that Our Lord will respond to with His saving love —

Follow Paul's example and let your feet take you into a church now and again so as to keep Our Lord company in His little box. But, if you are at death's door like the repentant thief, pray the words —

"Jesus, remember me . . . . !"

The Abiding City

MAY HE

Give us all the courage that we need to go
The way He shepherds us.
That when He calls,
That we may go unfrightened.
If He bids us come to Him across the waters,
That unfrightened we may go.
And if He bids us climb the hill,
May we not notice that it is a hill,
Mindful only of the happiness of His company.

He made us for Himself,
That we should travel with Him
And see Him at last In His unveiled beauty.
In The Abiding City where
He is light and happiness and endless home.

(Father Bede Jarratt OP)

"Life is only for LOVE

Time is only that we may FIND GOD."

(St. Bernard)

Finding God

My purpose is to give eternal life abundantly . . .

(John 10:10)

Dear reader, if your search for God flounders as it does for everyone at times, Jesus uses Paul, whom we met earlier, to teach us the way. With childlike trust he knew for certain that Jesus was actually in His little box and very lonely. Jesus' return visit confirms the fact He was where Paul believed Him to be. Imitate Paul and believe as he did that you have found The Hidden God in Jesus Christ His Son. It is not necessary to see Him.

Why Paul? Because he behaved like a little child and was humble and contrite. He prayed from the heart and in his simple way had found favour with Our Lord. God could have taken Paul up to heaven there and then and no one would be any the wiser. Had he died in hospital some would have thought 'He will get what he deserves.' But how wrong they would have been. We are all sinners and it does not pay to be judgmental – Judge not . . .! (Matt.7:1)

But no, Paul was cured and for a few short minutes in this life lived the Beatific Vision as a promise of it forever. The manner of his cure ensured the seed of a message of eternal life-giving importance was sown.

The message is this —

Jesus really suffers loneliness in His little box and longs for your company and mine.

He pleads with us to return the love He has shown to us, the whole human race, by His Cross, death and resurrection to save us all from our sins. It is clear that Jesus wants this message spread and acted upon.

He longs for the company of those with faith, those with little faith and those with none. Pay a visit to Our Lord in His little box. When you decide to leave His presence, your inner voice may say to you - "Do not go yet." So give in and stay a while! If you are stuck for words simply introduce yourself like Paul then say: "Dear Lord and God, be merciful to me a sinner."

"It is pleasant to spend time with Him, to be close to His heart like the Beloved Disciple and to feel the infinite love present in His heart. If in our time Christians must be distinguished by the Art of Prayer, how can we not feel a renewed need to spend time in spiritual converse, in silent adoration, in heartfelt love before Christ present in the Most Holy Sacrament. How often dear brothers and sisters, have I experienced this, and drawn from it strength, consolation and support."

(Pope John Paul II)

However, many are unable to follow Paul's and Pope John Paul's example of visiting Jesus in the Most Holy Sacrament in His little box there in the church. Are workers, merchant seamen, the housebound, the sick and the infirm therefore denied the chance of finding the Hidden God? Jesus gave us His answer to this problem on Pentecost Sunday when He filled His followers with God the Holy Spirit to dwell in them. The New Testament account of this is given on pages 37-38. The more prayerful you become, the more you sense and know that the God you are communing with is within your very own self. God is everywhere!

Here is a child-like morning and night prayer from the heart to the Holy Spirit whereby you will find God. Slowly but surely it will dawn on you that your prayer is being answered day by day and that The Holy Spirit is your friend and God and that your search is over. By His grace you have been shown the way. Then by prayer hold tightly on to God the Holy Spirit within. Remember to thank Him for His loving care.

Befriend Me Holy Spirit

Come, Holy Spirit befriend me.
Be with me each day in everything I do;
Be with me each night as I lift my heart to You;
Be with me each morn to greet me like the dew;
Be with me each time I'm weak instead of strong;
Befriend me Lord, my whole life long. Amen

(The Prayer Trust)

God made us to know Him, love and serve Him in this life and to be happy with Him in the next for eternity. Our final prayer expresses our innate longing to see God.

Contemplating Lord Thy hidden presence,
Grant me what I thirst for and implore,
In the revelation of Thine essence
To behold Thy Glory evermore.

(St. Thomas Aquinas)

Amen, Alleluia

It is truly right and fitting that this book closes with the following Scripture writings and the ones overleaf. Living Light will flood your path as you follow Our Lord Jesus Christ.

God loved the world so much that He gave His only Son so that anyone who believes in Him shall not perish but shall have eternal life. (John 3:16)

God . . . brought us back to Himself through what Christ Jesus did. And God has given us the privilege of urging everyone to come into favour and be reconciled to Him. For God was in Christ, restoring the world to Himself, no longer counting men's sins against them but blotting them out. This is the wonderful message He has given us to tell others. We are Christ's ambassadors. God is using us to speak to you: we beg you, as though Christ were here pleading with you, receive the love He offers you, be reconciled to God. For God took the sinless Christ and poured into Him our sins. Then in exchange, He poured God's goodness into us! (2 Corinthians 5:18-21)

God is Love: God showed us how much He loves us by sending His only Son into this wicked world to bring us to eternal life through His death. In this act we see what real love is: it is not our love for God, but His love for us when He sent His Son to satisfy God's anger against our sins. Dear friends, since God loved us as much as that, we surely ought to love each other too. (1 John 4:8-11)

God has given each of you some special abilities; be sure to use them to help each other, passing on to others God's many kinds of blessings. (1 Peter 4:10)

Deo Gratias!

DEUS CARITAS EST

No Greater Love . . . . .   (John 15:13)

I am the Way, the Truth and the Life.
(John 14:6)

**Finally, for you dear reader, the beautiful
Biblical Blessing from the Book of Numbers.**

The Lord bless you and keep you.

The Lord let His face shine upon you
and be gracious to you.

The Lord look upon you kindly
and give you peace.
(Num. 6: 24-26)

This book is a loving gift given to you by Instruments of Divine Providence who have donated in the name of Saint Joachim. If you want extra copies for friends, ask the kind person who gave you yours!

Dear Reader, having read your gift copy of this book, you may wish others to receive its message about prayer. If you feel disposed to help its distributors restock for further gifting of 'THE WAY OF LIGHT', please make a donation by cheque made payable to:-

SAINT JOACHIM'S PURSE
and send to the following address:-
Michael Radford, 11e Sussex Square, Brighton BN2 5AA

Saint Joachim and Saint Anne

These two saints were the parents of the Blessed Virgin Mary the Mother of Jesus the Son of God and Son of Man. Doubtless they spoilt their grandson as do all grandparents!

Saint Anne is a well known saint; Saint Joachim less so, in fact the mention of his name usually draws a blank look even from most Christians. This is a very sad state of affairs considering his role in Almighty God's scheme of salvation of the human race from their sins. Perhaps you yourself were also unaware of this great but silent saint. Reading this end paper note may have made good a gap in your knowledge. This is reason enough for owning this book!

By this simple way as Instruments of Divine Providence let us put the means into Saint Joachim's purse so he becomes known as the Saint who spoils his grandchildren in Christ. The gift we enable him to give to others may help unlock the door of a prayer life and help them to Heaven there to join his beloved daughter Mary and her Son Jesus, Our Saviour.